MARTIN WILLIAMS

Squiggle, Fiddle, Splat! 101 Genius Fine Motor And Early Writing Activities

Early Impact

Contents

II Early Writing Activities

Foreword

Your Free Book Is Waiting

How do you get children excited about numbers when playing outside? How can you inspire outstanding progress in mathematics through outdoor learning? How can you set up engaging activities on a limited budget?

This beautifully illustrated book provides 50 inspirational number activities for children aged 3 to 6.

Download For Free At This Link Below

https://earlyimpactbooks.com/50-games/

Download for free at – https://earlyimpactbooks.com/50-games/

Preface

There are quite a lot of books around that discuss the *why* of fine motor and early writing. Why it is so important. Why some children have issues. Why we should make it child-centred, and based around their current levels of learning. Why we should develop gross motor and then fine motor.

This book takes all this into account, but more importantly it addresses the *how*.

In particular...

How to get children interested.

How to get them making marks.

How to provide fine motor activities they simply cannot resist.

How to tap into their interests.

How to engage children that simply couldn't care less.

How to inspire boys in particular, and close the gender gap as much as is possible.

How to get everyone making marks out of other activities that come first.

How to create 'hooks'.

How to use superheroes, dinosaurs, unicorns, and all the other things that excite and enthuse.

The huge emphasis of this book is practical ideas (101 of them to be precise). However, it is probably a good idea to quickly look at the main barriers to fine motor and early writing learning, and a few tips on how to overcome these.

1. The Gender Gap

Nature has decreed that, generally speaking, girls develop fine motor skills at a quicker rate in the first few years than boys.

Across the world, the figures seem to suggest there is a gap of approximately 20% between the skills of boys and girls in this area by the time they reach 5.

There has always been a fine motor gulf, and always will be.

This cannot be avoided, and it is not a bad thing. It is just the way nature is.

The approach should be that it cannot be stopped, but it can be managed. The important thing is that boys are engaged and not put off. As long as they keep going, then they will 'catch up' at some point.

The danger is that they become disillusioned, and either give up or are at least slowed down.

But how can we overcome this?

Without over-simplifying things too much, there is one maxim to keep in mind throughout this book:

Engage the boys, and you engage everyone.

The majority of the activities in this book are created with boys in mind. Girls will definitely like them too, but I think boys will often lead the enthusiasm.

If the boys are learning, then the girls will be too. I hope this doesn't come across as sexism - it certainly is not intended to be. It just seems to be the way things are, backed up by many pieces of research.

So think diggers, superheroes, rockets, and all that kind of thing.

2. A Lack Of Enthusiasm

This is probably the key problem. There are many children that have less interest in fine motor or early writing than anything else in the curriculum.

There are a few children that adamantly resist trying it.

However, there are many more that are just quite indifferent. They are not anti-fine motor, or anti-making marks. They just aren't very interested.

I think this is the secret sauce of this book.

I have used the word 'genius' in the title on purpose, not just as some cynical ploy to get you to buy the book (honestly). I think that the best fine motor and early writing activities contain that little spark of something extra to get the children engaged.

Run-of-the-mill stuff doesn't really cut it in this area.

It ideally needs to be something amusing, entertaining, scintillating.....that ignites their curiosity and gets them wanting to do it in a way that they can't resist.

Tapping into interests is massive where fine motor and early writing is concerned. I would say it's more important than in any other area of early education.

If they're not interested in the theme or activity content, many will be reluctant in a way that you'll not see when they try other areas of the curriculum.

However, all children are interested in *something*. It is all about targeting those cracks in their curiosity, and then piling into them when they have been located.

Most children need ideas to get them started. Open-ended play works well when they have a foundation of ideas and images in their minds to build from.

However, getting to that point is the challenge!

3. Lack Of Budget

I hear a lot of teachers talking about a lack of budget in general, and this has a big impact on the resources you can get, and the amount of adults available.

These are definitely big issues, and will continue to be.

Luckily, however, everything in this book is either free or extremely cheap. You do not have to break the bank to have success in fine motor or early writing – quite the opposite probably.

Many of the activities use the simplest resources that you probably have already, or that you could find very quickly. With a few pots of play dough, some sticks, tweezers, stones, and a few other things, you can quickly conjure up a whole array of high-quality and imaginative learning experiences.

A Quick Overview Of The Book

In terms of structure, I have simply split the book into two. The first half is approximately fifty fine-motor activities, and the second half is early writing games (hopefully fifty-one).

There is a lot of overlap of skills, and some writing can take place in the fine motor games, and vice versa.

The fine motor section describes activities that can be done by children certainly between the ages of 3-5, but could also be done by many two year olds as well. Also, there are lots of activities that could have large benefits for children aged 6,7, or older.

The early writing segment of the book describes activities that you can do to stimulate learning in between two key points: the first is when children start making marks, and the end point is beginning to write letters and words. These activities bridge the huge time-span between these two events.

I think, in general, children should do a lot more fine motor activities than early writing between the ages of 2 to at least 4 (and possibly a bit older). Around about 4-5, I think it is good to have a balance of both. And from 5 onwards I think writing should start to happen a bit more than fine motor.

This will of course depend massively on individual children, and also which country you are working in. However, this is a rough benchmark, and something to bear in mind when you put these games into action.

In a career of more than ten years of teaching children aged 3-5, I have been continually scouting for fine motor and early writing activities that brought that extra *something* that seemed so necessary. These secret activities seemed harder to come by than they did in all the other areas of the curriculum.

After having tried hundreds and possibly thousands of activities, I unearthed some pure gems that seemed to pretty much work every time.

These seem to have that allure, that excitement attached to them, that got children engaged and learning. These are the subject of this book.

Quick Safety Notice

Before we get going, a quick word about safety.

Fine motor and early writing are definitely not particularly dangerous areas of the early education curriculum. However, the most important thing to be aware of is choking.

Fine motor learning is based around small objects, and there is always a risk that children will try to put these in their mouths.

To manage this risk, and having sought professional advice from a health and safety expert, I have put together these very simple '3 Golden Rules' before we start. These are certainly not rocket science just to warn you! But they are just simple pointers to adhere with to make sure these activities will be as safe as possible when trying them out.

The 3 Golden Rules are:

1.When purchasing small objects, make sure items are age-appropriate, and follow any age specifications from manufacturers (e.g. if using pompoms with 3 year olds, make sure they state that they are OK to be used with this age on the packaging)

2.Risk assess the level of supervision that is required for any particular resource or activity

3.Tidy away all small parts that have been used after an activity or session has finished (including any stray objects on the floor etc)

Right, now that's out of the way, let's dive into the good and juicy content of this book, starting with some spectacular fine motor activities.

I

Fine Motor Activities

1

Pipette Activities

If you try only one thing out of this book, a great choice would be some of these pipette activities.

The excitement created by pipettes is immense!

I would recommend getting biggish ones if you can. The ones I have now are 5ml pipettes. You can even get much larger for very young children. I get the medical pipettes, which are super cheap to say the least.

Pipettes are fantastic for pincer grip, squeezing, using the muscles in your fingers, physical development, hand-eye coordination, and just generally for squirting different substances during a range of fun games.

1. Bathtub Mats

This first activity is really bizarre, but definitely a real cracker.

All you need is a bathtub mat, one that has plenty of round suction pads in its underside.

What you then need is some pots of coloured water. A mixture of mainly water with a little bit of paint mixed in is perfect for this. Food colouring would also work, but there would be a risk of staining clothes. I stick to washable paint.

I normally use the primary colours – red, blue and yellow.

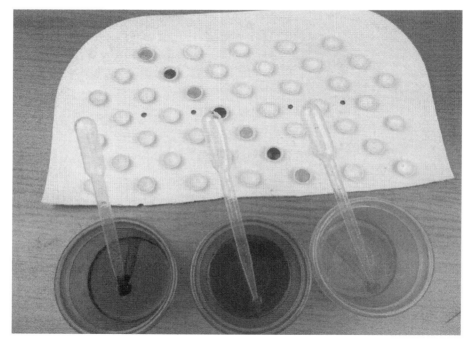

A section of a bath mat, coloured water and pipettes. Fantastically random fun

The idea is that the children get a pipette, dip it into the coloured water and squeeze. They suck up some water and then squirt it into the suction pads of the bath-mat. Truly bizarre, but very therapeutic.

There are many more structured things that you can do (which we'll come to in a minute), but in its very simplest form, it's good to let the children just explore with this activity and see what happens.

There are many things to experience, and this bath-mat idea contains multiple possibilities in one resource.

One of these is colour mixing. This will happen spontaneously if the children are left to explore, but could also be done in a more structured way. It is simple – just squirt one colour into a suction pad, and then add a bit of another. If you use primary colours, you can create lots of vivid oranges, greens and purples.

Another idea is repeated patterns. For example, you can create a line of coloured suction pads going 'red, yellow, red, yellow'. More skilful children can attempt more varied patterns, using three or more colours, or more complex sequences (such as 'red, red, yellow, red, red, yellow.')

Repeating patterns

Connect Four is a possibility!

This is another one for children probably from about five upwards. A two player game is simplest. The players have one colour each, and they take it in turns to squirt that colour into a suction pad.

The idea is the first player to get four of their colour in a row is the winner. This is excellent for problem solving, turn-taking, and simple counting (as well as fine motor being a real winner as well of course).

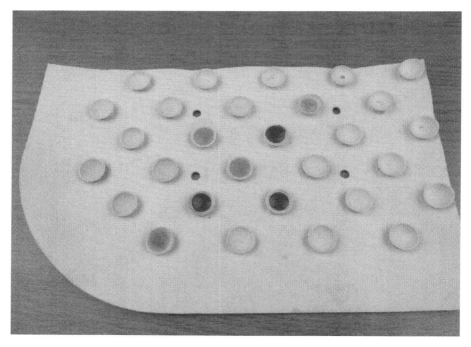

Connect Four

This bath-mats idea is extremely addictive, and some children will play with them over an extended period. Seeing children achieve this state of 'flow', and 'getting in the zone', is where the highest-quality learning will be happening.

2. Ice Cube Trays And Duplo

There are many other things that you can probably find that you can also squirt coloured water into using pipettes.

Ice cube trays are fantastic for this. It is especially good if you can find one with ten sections, as then it becomes a fun ten-frame.

Upside-down pieces of Duplo work well also. Duplo has the little round columns underneath it that you can try to squirt into. This is quite a trickier experience than the bath-mats.

Other objects you could use include:
   i) Egg cups
   ii) Shot glasses (the plastic ones)
   iii) Cake tins
   iv) Any kind of tray split up into sections

3. Ten Frames/Five Frames

Back to bathtub-mats now.

The idea of this activity is that you cut some sections out of the bath-mat.

For example, cut out five suction pads in a row to create a five-frame, like this:

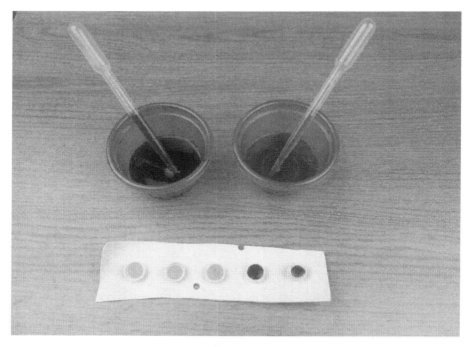

A five frame

To create a ten-frame, cut out a rectangular grid five suction pads long and two high.

Five and ten frames provide a wonderful way of helping children to visualise numbers and quantities in the context of ten.

You can try all sorts of fabulous number games with these DIY frames and a selection of coloured water pots, some examples being:

i) Create numbers in different arrays. For example, in what ways can you make the number four?

ii) Copy the Numicon piece

iii) Adding – add three blue plus two red for example

iv) Number bonds. For example, if you have six red pads, how many yellow will you need to make ten?

v) Repeating patterns

vi) Just simple exploration of pattern, quantity and number

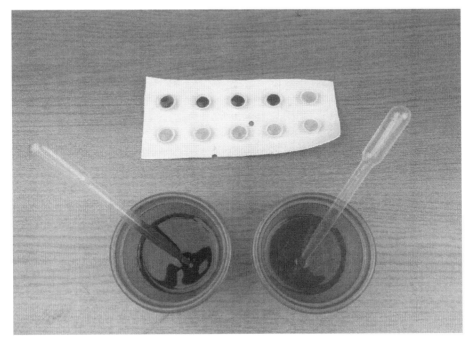

A ten frame

There is so much going on! So simple and engaging.

4. Subtraction

One great trick that they really enjoy is first squeeze a pipette, and then place it into a suction pad full of coloured liquid. Then release the squeeze, and the pipette sucks the liquid out of the suction pad. Some children will do this for an extremely extended period, and really get 'in the zone'.

This technique lends itself well to subtraction.

It would be a great one to do with either the ten frames or the five frames, so they can see the subtraction calculation in the context of five or ten.

For example, if you were trying to find 4 subtract three, you would first fill four suction pads in a five or ten frame bath mat. Then you suck three suctions pads back out so they are empty. How many do you have left?

A very visual and fun way of combining calculating and fine motor.

5. Jackson Pollock Art

This is probably best outside, as it can be spectacularly messy!

You've probably seen Jackson Pollock paintings, but if not just google him. They use predominantly dripping and splashing of paint to produce a range of effects, often in a structured way, or using a certain colour palette.

They are a perfect stimulus for largescale and enjoyable mark-making.

Get a large surface, such as a huge piece of wallpaper, or something like an old white bedsheet would be perfect for the job too.

Then get the same kind of gear that we used for the bath-mats – coloured water in different pots, and some pipettes.

The children squeeze, splash and generally 'let rip' on the big surface. They create all sorts of drizzles, squirts, spatter-marks, splashes – the full Jackson Pollock experience.

Jackson Pollock art

This is so much fun that no child would ever think that it is linked to fine motor, mark-making, or 'work' in any kind of way.

You can also attempt this vertically.

Place a sheet or wallpaper on a wall, and unleash in the same kind of way. This creates a dripping effect also.

For either ways of doing it, you can also use larger squirting devices if you are feeling brave. Turkey basters would be great for this, and they are basically like giant pipettes.

Water guns are another possibility. This will just require a good level of supervision so that things do not degenerate into a paint war.

I visited a school recently that said they kept their sheets out on the wall all the time. They said the rain naturally washes a lot of colour away from the sheets.

We do get a lot of rain in the UK, and this probably wouldn't work in a drier climate, but if you can do it where you are then this would be a great way to have large mark-making as part of play all the time.

6. Oil On A Plate

This is a beautiful art exploration that goes hand-in-hand with fine motor development.

You need some cooking oil (of any type) and some kind of surface to put the oil onto.

I use paper plates, as these are extremely simple to dispose of afterwards. If you feel this is not that eco-friendly, you could potentially use something that you just wash at the end. A real plate would work. Just bear in mind that washing all the oil off the plates is a big and time-consuming job.

This is another activity that is great outside on something like grass, as this really minimises the effect of any oil spillages.

Place a thin layer of oil in some paper plates. All that is required is just enough to cover the surface of the plate.

Then the children will squirt coloured droplets of water onto the oil.

The effect is like a lava lamp – they create beautiful round blobs that are completely separated from the oil.

There are all sorts of effects you can create. You can make swirls, by skimming the pipette through the blobs. You can colour mix, by squirting different tones into the blobs on the plate. You can create patterns and lines and blobs of different sizes.

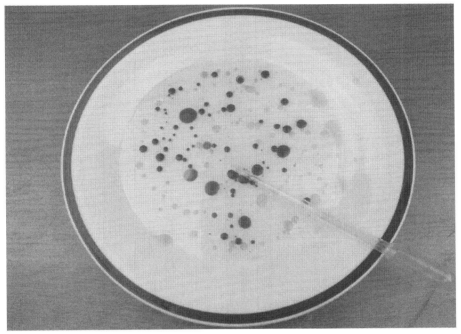

Create beautiful effects using oil on a plate (either a paper-plate for a quick tidy-away, or use a real one like in the picture if you don't mind a bit of washing)

This is a beautiful stimulus for talk and discussion.

It is also excellent for artistic experimentation and visual creativity.

If you are feeling very ambitious, you could try this on a large surface. Something like the base of a large water tray would be perfect.

Or you could spread out a huge piece of cling-film.

Just be aware of the washing that is required at the end if it is something you can't throw away.

7. Snow

This is a simple and beautiful fine motor activity to try whenever it snows.

Realistically I would not try this the first time it snows in your area. Children are so excited then that the last thing they want to do is go out with pipettes.

Simple snow activities and play are definitely the way to experience snow when it first starts falling.

Pipettes are more something to use if you have an extended period of snow on the ground, when you are looking for more imaginative ways to interact with it.

Take some coloured water and pipettes out into the snow, and simply fire the colours at the snow.

The colours will blossom out in beautiful effects! Excellent for colour mixing, and talking about visual experiences.

8. Absorbent Materials

There are all sorts of materials that you can use with pipettes that are excellent for absorbing colours, and creating different artistic effects.

Kitchen paper is good for this. Squirt colour onto it, and it will blossom out in a spectacular way.

Cotton wool balls are a fun one for this as well. We made spooky 'eyeballs' by simply squiring a blob of red into the middle of each cotton ball. This made them look like blood-shot eyeballs.

A gruesome, blood-stained eye-ball - mwah ha ha!

Sheets of cotton wool are even more versatile. They work in a similar way to kitchen paper, with the colours blossoming out from where they land.

9. Fizzy Ice!

This is a fantastic fine motor science activity.

The idea is to get some ice cubes or crushed ice, and some baking soda. Mix the baking soda into the ice.

Then get some vinegar. Use pipettes to suck up the vinegar, and then squirt it onto the ice.

The ice will fizz! Another great one for communication, excitement and talk, whilst all the fabulous fine motor development will be going on below the surface.

2

Play Dough Sports

There are so many children that are passionate about sports of some description, and if you can get these into early education it usually creates fantastic results.

In the UK there are a huge number of football (soccer) addicts, but there are probably other sports that predominate in other countries in the world.

Get fine motor into football activities, and you get these football-addicts hooked.

These play dough sports are also extremely boy-friendly, and will hopefully tempt some of those harder to reach children.

A few of these activities I'm about to describe are football-related, but I think just a bit of creativity would be required to change the focus to cricket or baseball, or whatever other sports your children are into.

1. Play Dough Football (Soccer)

This is one of the ultimate fine motor activities, and one that can hook some children for hours.

It is good played on a large tuff-spot, a play tray, or some kind of similar large tray. This stops the ball from flying off!

You could play it on a table-top, but just be prepared for balls whizzing across the floor.

You make a goal (or the children make goals). Lolly (popsicle) sticks work well for this with some play dough. Get a ball of dough and place a stick in it vertically. This is a goal-post. You need two for a goal (obviously).

If you are going to do a competitive game, then you need two goals, one at each end of the tuff-spot or play-tray.

Then you get some kind of ball. This could be a ping-pong ball, a pompom, or a play dough ball works really well. Just mould a ball of dough into a smallish ball shape.

Now you need some footballers. Lolly sticks are perfect for this jobs as well.

The children hold the 'footballers' and try to kick the ball around the pitch.

There's different ways of doing it. They could be playing against each other, and each trying to score in the other's goal. Or they could team up and try to score in one goal together.

This is so simple, but excellent for a range of skills. The children develop strength in their fingers, hand-eye coordination, pincer grip, muscle development in the fingers and hands, as well as there being many other benefits. All this is happening in secret, with the big emphasis for them being on an exciting game of mini-football.

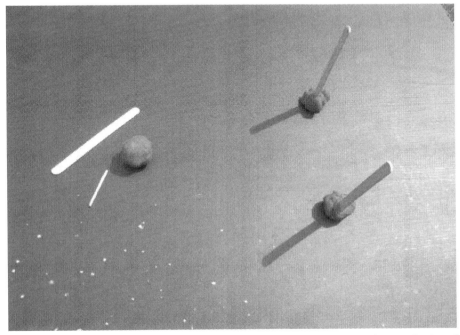

Play dough football is so simple. Just a couple of goals, a ball and a 'footballer' and away you go. Warning – highly addictive

You can make the game harder or easier depending on the age and level of challenge required by the children.

Younger children can use really wide lolly (popsicle) sticks, whereas more skilful children could use something like a little matchstick for a much trickier fine motor experience.

If you keep score, this experience of counting for a purpose is great for a range of number skills, including:

    i) Knowing which number is bigger (because that person is winning)

    ii) Finding one more (whenever you score)

    iii) One to one correspondence

    iv) Knowing how many more (for example, if you have 4 and your friend has 2 goals, how many more do you have?)

2. Non-Competitive Version

Of course this game can definitely be done in a range of non-competitive ways as well.

One great example of this is to use loose parts.

Get some random objects, such as stones, corks, leaves, or anything else like that, and put them around the 'pitch'. This is like an obstacle course.

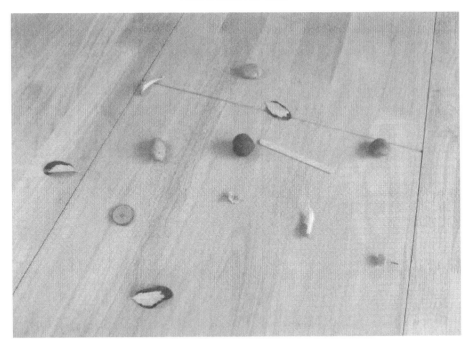

A loose parts obstacle course

The children can then try to 'dribble' one ball each around the obstacles without touching them. The dribbling is just basically tapping and rolling the ball with the stick.

They can create their own obstacle courses which creates an added element of creativity. They could incorporate things like ramps or tunnels maybe, using blocks or whatever else they think of.

Another way of doing the non-competitive version is to do 'football drills'. For example, get the lumps of dough with sticks in them that you used for the goals and rearrange them in a line. These are the 'cones' that the footballers will try to dribble around.

3. Penalty Shoot-Outs

A great simple version of the playdough football game is to have a penalty shoot-out.

One goal is required, one ball, and two stick footballers.

One player is shooting first, the other is in goal. Have five shots and then swop places.

This game is excellent for many early number skills, such as:
   i) One to one correspondence
   ii) Counting for a purpose
   iii) Number bonds. I would say this is the key skill that it teaches. If you have five shots, and miss two, you will have scored three. This practical way of encountering number bonds really gets children *experiencing* what they are. The repetition is good to build mental recall also
   iv) Recording numbers. You can write down your score, or at least draw a few dots or make some marks
   v) Understanding more/less. You need to score more to win, so this really strengthens this concept in their minds

4. Add Extra Resources

Here are just a few ways of extending the play dough football theme even more, before going on to some different sports.

One way is to find the faces of famous footballers (from newspapers, or printed from the internet), cut them out and stick them on the lolly sticks.

This really adds to engagement. Try to make it relevant to the individual children. If you have some Manchester City fans, for example, put some of their players on, as well as balancing it out with rival teams.

Another way of doing it is to put numbers on the sticks. This is a good introduction to ordinal numbers.

5. Other Play Dough Sports

Play dough football is fantastic, but it is very much only the tip of the iceberg.

There are so many other options, and there will be many more I am sure you can think of as well. Some other great sports include:

i) Ten-pin bowling! Create some pins in a similar way to the football goals – balls of play dough with sticks placed vertically in them. Put a few in a formation and try to knock them over by rolling a large play dough ball at them. This is another fantastic one for number bonds. If you have five and knock down three, you will have two left.

ii) Tennis – This is a beautiful game of cooperation. Have one stick each, one ball, and hit it back and forwards to each other

iii) 'Air hockey' – This is very similar to playdough football, maybe just with some kind of zone to score in that is larger than the football goal

iv) Cricket or baseball – One child rolls the ball, the other child tries to hit it. Do this a few times then swap over

v) Catapult! Make catapult seesaws by balancing lolly sticks on balls of play dough, and try to propel dough balls through the air!

6. Golf

I thought golf deserved its own section in this chapter, because it is great fun, and also a game that can be adapted in multiple ways.

A simple way to play playdough golf is that you first create some kind of golf course. A huge piece of wallpaper on the floor is ideal.

Draw some large circles on the paper. These are the golf 'holes'. The idea is you get a ball (a dough ball, pompom, or something similar) and also a lolly/popsicle stick that is going to be the golf club. Place the ball wherever you want on the golf course, and then try to hit it towards a hole. Count your shots before you get the ball inside the circle.

'Golf' can be adapted in many different ways

This can be adapted in multiple ways, including:

i) Label the golf holes with numbers. This is good for number recognition, and you can also go in order as well (like a real golf course!)

ii) Put sounds or words on the holes. Great for phonics games

iii) Have differently shaped holes – e.g. a triangle, square, pentagon etc. Good for recognising shapes

iv) Combine the numbers with mathematical challenges. For example, say 'what is one more than three'. The children try to work out the problem, and hit the ball to the correct hole.

3

Unicorns

For many children, unicorns are literally the most exciting thing on Planet Earth.

Therefore, if you can combine unicorns and fine motor in some way, you will have created a rich source of endless enthusiasm and interest.

I also wanted to add a little balance to this book. There are a huge number of activities targeted at the harder to motivate boys.

These unicorn games add something different to the mix. Many girls will really love them, but of course there will be many boys that do too. The fourth idea in the chapter suggests a few ways you can make the activity more 'boy-friendly' if you need to.

1. Fine Motor Unicorns

There really are so many ways you can make unicorns that are great for fine motor, but here are some great ways to start.

Get a lump of play dough each, and the children shape it into something that looks a bit like a unicorn's head. They can be really artistic if they want to and add googly eyes and a multi-coloured mane, and anything else like that if they want to.

However, that is completely optional, because the true fine-motor skills come in when they create the unicorn's horn!

There are many things you can use for a unicorn's horn, but something like a lolly (popsicle) stick would be ideal. You could also use a wooden skewer or a twig.

Now you are going to jazz up the horns to look really magical.

One way is to use mini loom-bands. These are a bit out of fashion these days, and you can pick up a bag for almost nothing. They are little circular rubber bands if you've not seen them.

The children put the small loom bands on the unicorn's horn. When you get lots on there they stack up, and also look all magical and sparkly, like a real unicorn's horn!

Mini-loom bands are a fantastic and fiddly object to create beautiful unicorn horns

Another way of doing it is to get pieces of coloured material such as wool or ribbon. Each piece should be roughly twice the length of the horn.

Put two blobs of playdough at each end of the material, and then fix one to the top of the horn. The idea is that you wind the material round the horn as you go down it, before splodging the end piece of dough into the unicorn's head.

Weaving to create a unicorn horn

It looks a bit like a may-pole.

This is kind of like a DIY weaving activity. When you get a few pieces of material on there, once again it looks all magical and multi-coloured, like a genuine unicorn horn!

There are other very simple ways of jazzing up the horns. You can draw patterns on the sticks with felt tip pens. Or you can stick sequins onto them with glue. So easy to set up, and just something that many children want to do anyway.

2. 'Old School' Fine Motor Unicorns

There are many 'old school' fine motor activities that have been known and loved, that can be adapted for unicorns and given a new lease of life.

One of these is the cheerios on the skewer game.

You've probably played or seen this one. A skewer is now the unicorn's horn, and you put some cheerios onto it. If you can get cheerios in two or three different colours you can make patterns as well. This activity is really energised and brought to life so much more if it is a unicorn's horn!

The same could be done using beads or small wooden rings. You could also use something like smallish curtain hooks.

Another idea is using a long bolt and some cogs. Have a ball of playdough for the head again, and press the bolt into the dough so that the end is sticking out up into the air. Spin some cogs onto the bolt. Hours of unicorn fun!

One last idea is to use pipe-cleaners. Twist them around the horns in a spiral going up or down.

3. Pasta Unicorns

This is another idea that draws on an old activity, but revitalises it by adapting it for use with unicorns.

Have something like a thin stick or skewer for the unicorn horn, and then some tubes of pasta. There are many games you can do, the simplest being that the children put the tubes onto the horn from bottom to top. This is definitely the way to start with young children.

Old fine motor activities like pasta tubes on a skewer are really revitalised by adding the unicorn element.

If you get two different colours of pasta tubes (or possibly paint them two different colours) you then have a few more options at your disposal to extend this activity, such as:

i) You can create repeating patterns – e.g. red, green, red, green

ii) If you are feeling ambitious you can try addition. It could be three green add two red for example. You could generate numbers by using a dice, and then finding the answer

iii) You can find one more – e.g. put four pieces of pasta on, and then find out what one more would be

4. Dinosaurs, Bulls, And Other Variations

There are some children that are not massively keen on unicorns and ponies, but luckily these games are very adaptable into other forms.

Pretty much the same models, for example, could be:
    i) A dinosaur, particularly triceratops with a long nose
    ii) A rhino
    iii) A bull with two long horns (use two sticks rather than one)
    iv) A stag
    All the earlier unicorn games would work perfectly in these new guises.

A triceratops?!

4

Stepping Stones Games

Here are few games that really channel huge interests for most children into some simple challenges and activities.

They centre around two of the ultimate parts of life – Spiderman, and the floor is lava! If you know anything more exciting than either of these then I'd love to hear about it.

All the games can be played in a very simple way, or you can expand them with numerous resources and options.

Here we go...

1. Floor Is Lava! (Mini Version)

For many children this is the greatest pastime – pretending the floor is lava. You will see children playing it in shops, as they walk down the street, or as they play outside. Cracks can be lava, or differently coloured paving slabs can be.

The idea is to take this passion for 'lava-play' (if that is really even a thing), and use it on a small scale.

Have some kind of surface that is the 'lava'. It could be a table top or a tuff-spot or play-tray, for example.

You can leave the surface as it is, or you could really go for it and jazz it up with something red or orange, such as big paper. This gives the impression of it being real lava.

The idea of the game is to build a path or walkway across the lava. You cannot touch it of course! However, you can place stepping-stones over it and balance things on them.

You can use many different things for the stepping-stones. It could be small balls of play dough, for example. You could also use corks, bottle tops, or flat stones.

Whatever you use, simply place them in a spaced-out line across the lava, and then try to balance things over them to make a bridge or walkway.

This activity is great for spatial awareness and problem solving. Children start to understand how far the stepping stones need to be apart to make it work – not too far apart, or the things won't balance, but also not too close either.

Good resources for the bridge are things like lolly sticks, twigs, straws, or something else similar to that. A mixture of resources for both the stepping-stones and the bridge is ideal, as this really gets the children thinking and problem solving.

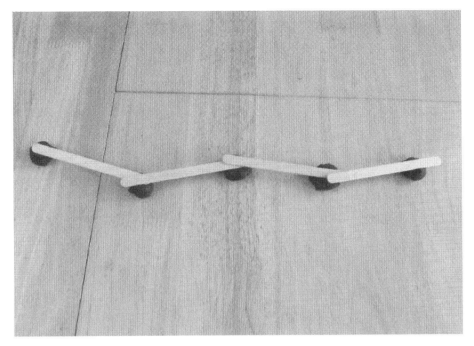

The floor is lava! Make a bridge using whatever you can find

When we tried this last, we also made little mini-people out of loose parts and playdough and walked them across the walkway. This really brought it to life. A bit of storytelling and narrative brings added depth to pretty much all play experiences.

2. Bridge Over The Troll's River

This is very much an adaptation of the 'Floor Is Lava' game above.

This is a beautiful narrative retelling of 'The Three Billy Goats Gruff', with fine motor very much at the fore.

Have a similar set-up, only now the surface on which you do the activity is not going to be lava, but the troll's river. Some kind of blue surface might well work to demonstrate this, though this is definitely not essential. Getting children to fill in gaps with their imagination is absolutely fine and arguably even preferable.

Use a range of resources for the goats to build a bridge across the river.

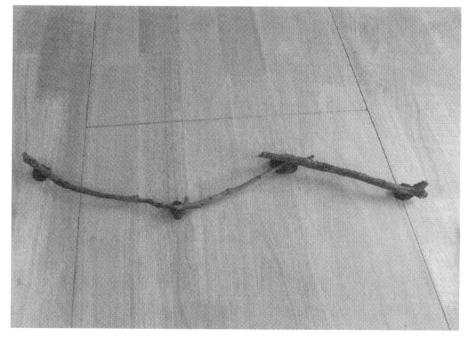

A bridge over the troll's river

You can then really bring it to life by getting them to create mini-goats and walking across the bridge. Acting out the story, and taking on the voices of characters really adds to the experience.

3. Make Spiderman's Webs

Here we go with an absolute classic – making Spiderman's webs!

For some children, Spiderman is just about as exciting as it can ever get, and this activity taps into this enthusiasm to engage them in a multi-layered fine motor experience.

The general principle is pretty similar to the 'floor is lava' game.

Any simple table-top, or even the ground will work fine (no jazzing it up in any way is required).

You put a random array of 'stepping-stones' all over the place in a small space. These could be play dough balls, or corks, flat stones, bottle-tops, or any of that kind of thing.

Then you balance twigs, or lolly sticks, matchsticks, or straws all over the stepping stones in a mish-mash, interweaving pattern.

Keep doing this, and it always looks a bit like a spider's web in the end – I promise you!

Spiderman's web – criss-cross lots of sticks across balls of dough or bottle tops, and it always looks like a web in the end (honestly)

Another great one for dexterity, hand-eye coordination and physical development, all fuelled by the Spiderman passion driving them on.

4. Making Shapes

This is another derivative of the same kinds of resources and principles used in the last few games.

Get some stepping stones, and place them out to make 2D shapes, such as squares, triangles, pentagons, and the like. Then balance sticks on them to create the shapes.

Here are two simple 2D shapes, but you could make all sorts of things

Great for the following:

i) Making more complex shapes with more skilful children

ii) Making simple writing patterns such as zig-zags (a lot more about this later)

iii) Creating pictures, e.g. a house

iv) Problem solving. For example, if you have a square, how can you turn it into a shape with one more side?

v) Making 'silly' shapes, that have lots of sides, or an irregular shape

vi) Adding an element of storytelling to your creation, for example making a castle wall (as a random example!)

5

Posting Games

All you need to try out any of the activities in this chapter are just a few random recycled boxes, tubes or cartons.

These games are all fantastic for children that love posting things! Any available slot and they are posting all your best stuff into it. There are a huge number of children that love posting things, as I am sure you have witnessed in many ways.

Combine this passion with lots of lovely fine motor skills and you can't really go wrong.

1. Feed The Box

Get some kind of boxes (something like empty cereal boxes would be perfect). Then you cut a small circular hole in the box, about an inch across, though you could also go a bit smaller.

The box is going to be something that likes eating a lot. It could be:
   i) A tiger

ii) An alien

iii) A monster

iv) A zombie

v) A shark

Or anything else that you can think of in a similar vein.

The hole is the mouth, and you are going to be feeding whatever it is.

An optional way to jazz the box up a bit is to stick some kind of fake head on the box. I made ones with alien's heads on, as an example. This is very quick to do, and just adds a bit to the magic. Here's one of mine:

Feed the alien!

Now for the game. There are different ways of doing it, but the basic idea is you are going to feed something into the mouth of the box.

Play dough is brilliant for this. You can make little balls of 'food' and feed the box.

There are many ways this can be done, but a way that many children really like is to have a bit of a competition.

Get some kind of egg timer – something around 30 seconds is perfect. One child goes first. They have a lump of dough and the box they are going to feed.

They have thirty seconds to create and feed as many pieces of 'food' into the box as they can.

Then their friend will have a go at trying to beat their score. You can either count as you put them in the box, or count the balls of food at the end. Take your pick.

I find for some children a little bit of an element of fun competition like this can really help.

There are many children that are not massively interested in fine motor activities. If you ask them to thread something, or try weaving or whatever it is, they are just not interested.

However, if you are trying to beat your friend it can be a different story.

If your friend Charlie got six pieces of food into the alien's mouth, you want to go all out and get more!

Competition is not for everyone at this age, but it does have benefits such as:
   i) It is good for many harder to reach boys. It acts as a powerful motivator (for some)

ii) It is a good way to get an activity going. Try it in a competitive way first, and then explore non-competitive versions later

iii) It is good for 1:1 counting. It really promotes accurate counting, as children need to learn this or they are 'cheating' in the game (and their friends will notice and will also let them know all about it)

iv) It is great for understanding more and less (because you need 'more' to win)

2. Treasure Game

The treasure game is a very similar idea to the feed the box game.

Instead of feeding a hungry being, this time the box or carton you use is a treasure chest, and you are filling it with 'treasure' (whatever that may be).

For this I found some paper pirate cups in a local shop, but any kind of simple box, carton or cup would be fine. Cut a hole in the top.

A simple cup can become a 'treasure chest' with just a bit of creativity

Now you can play all the same kinds of games that you did before.

Post 'treasure' into it, either against the clock or not (whichever you prefer). Small dough balls once again are perfect.

The treasure chests are slightly easier to post things in than the bigger cereal boxes. Larger boxes require two hands, whereas smaller pots with a hole in the top can be successfully filled with just one hand.

3. Non-Competitive Posting Games

Of course, there are many ways of trying these posting games without the need for competition.

Some great ideas include:

i) Have a selection of different 'foods' that the box-monster can eat. It could be beans, pasta, dried spaghetti, and anything else like this

ii) Create secret 'messages' of some sort and post them into the box's mouth

iii) Have a menu. It could have pictures of what to feed the box, plus the quantity as well. For example, there could be a picture of pasta, and the number 4 next to it. Older children could potentially work out number problems – for example, 'pasta' and '4+3'

iv) Create a 'family' of boxes with differently sized holes (i.e. a giant hole for the biggest box etc)

v) Have multiple holes in one box of different sizes

A delicious feast of loose parts for this alien on a box to eat

4. Children Create Their Own

Of course any activity is greatly enhanced if the children have the opportunity to take ownership.

Children could design their own boxes in all sorts of imaginative ways. They can paint them, or stick things on them.

They can design their own character box, and then do many of the following things:

   i) Give it a name

   ii) Give it a funny voice

iii) Give a back-story

iv) Imagine what it likes to eat

v) Draw or write a menu of foods it likes to eat

Children can also find the 'food' or 'treasure' for their boxes.

Scouting round outside can help unearth all sorts of hidden gems that are great for posting.

So many possibilities!

6

Treasure Balls

There is something quite magical about finding objects that are hidden inside something else.

This concept has an allure and an element of secrecy about it. There are all the questions: how did the objects get in there? Where have they come from? How can we get them out? How can we hide our own objects?

This simple idea can lead to multiple fine motor ideas.

Pretty much all you need is some kind of substance and something that you can hide inside it and you are good to go. Children will take ages picking things out, using tongs, and generally fiddling and poking and tearing: the perfect formula for fine motor development.

Here's some great ways to try it...

1. Play Dough Treasure Balls

This is one of the best ways of doing this activity, and you can link it to all sorts of different skills.

In its simplest form, all you need is a ball of play dough (or several balls), and something hidden inside them. Some good things to put in are:

    i) Little pieces of paper screwed up. They could have sounds or numbers on

    ii) Small objects like shells or gems

    iii) Small objects that link to a theme or topic. At Christmas, there could be small decorations like sequins or something similar inside, for example. Basically anything small enough to stick into the balls that vaguely links to the topic is good for this

A simple treasure ball with the numerals 0–6 about to be screwed up and hidden inside it

It really helps if the balls have some kind of back-story attached to them. This adds to the interest that they generate. Storytelling in general in one of the best ways of getting children (and indeed adults) interested in anything.

The balls could have been sent by pirates from the pirate kingdom. Or they might have been delivered by aliens from their spaceship overnight. Or they could have sent in the post by a baddie in a story you are reading at that time.

Wherever they come from, just make something up, and this will exponentially improve the level of engagement.

The children are the treasure hunters. They are going to try to find whatever it is that is stuck in the treasure ball, and free it. In it's simplest form that is what they are going to try to do.

They can pick the objects out with their fingers, or they could use tweezers, tongs, chopsticks, or whatever else you have that might work.

2. Different Games With The Objects

Once the children have got whatever object it is out of the treasure ball, there is all sorts of things they can do with them.

I would say for very young children, getting things out should be the primary focus. But for children developing a range of further skills, then having a secondary objective is a good way to go. Getting the objects out in the first place is the creative 'hook', and the secondary activity is where lots of further learning takes place.

This game is great for numbers. You could have the numbers from 0 to 10 written on small pieces of screwed up paper for example. Children could:

i) Put them in order

ii) Find the numbers that unlock some kind of 'code'. Have a simple 'code' written on a piece of paper on the wall, and they try to match it. They could also create their own code and challenge others to find it in the treasure ball

iii) Older children could attempt finding one more or one less of numbers they find in the ball

iv) They could add numbers

v) You could have numbers in a sequence in 2s, 5s, or 10s, and the children put them in order

So many possibilities!

The numbers don't need to be just on pieces of paper. They could also be drawn with permanent marker on buttons, or onto sequins.

You could do a similar thing with letters. Put some letters on small pieces of paper, buttons or sequins, and then the children can try some of the following:

i) Recognise the letters

ii) Create 'code' words that you have written on a piece of paper on the wall

iii) Create secret sentences – either their own or again some that have been thought out ahead of time

iv) You could put simple three-letter words or sight words into the treasure balls as well to help them practise reading these

Of course, not everything should be about letters and number, and there are many other things you could put into the treasure balls. These could be:

i) Secret symbols

ii) Interesting objects – such as a range of different shells

iii) Jewels to make jewellery

iv) Little mini stones with images on

The list would be pretty much endless.

3. Different Substances

Of course using play dough is just one way of attempting this activity.

Any kind of messy substance will probably work well, depending on what objects you are going to put into it.

A trough of porridge oats is excellent for hiding any kind of thing inside.

If you want to go a bit messier, you can try one of the following:
 i) Shaving gel
 ii) Shaving foam
 iii) Gloop
 iv) Sand
 v) Mud
 vi) Soil

None of these are great for hiding paper in, as it will go muddy and self-destruct.

However, you can hide harder objects in these things. You can pick them out with fingers, or use tweezers, tongs, or all that kind of thing again.

7

Clothes Pins (Pegs) Games

Clothes pins (or 'pegs' as they are called in the UK) are a fantastic tool in your fine motor armoury.

They tick so many boxes – they are ridiculously cheap, and extremely plentiful, making it simple to get your hands on them with little effort. Also, they are great for squeezing, for pincer grip, for engaging all the muscles in the fingers, and generally working miracles for fine motor development.

But what do you do with them when you've got them?

The following clothes pins/pegs activities are real gems, and pretty much guaranteed to tap into the curiosity of most children. Here we go...

1. Making Trees

For this activity you need as a bare minimum a lump of dough, some clothes pins, and some kind of stick. There are many more optional resources you could use, as we will see.

Each child has one lump of play dough or plasticine and puts it on the table.

Then they need some kind of trunk for the tree. This could be a lolly (popsicle) stick for a smaller effect, or it could be something like a long twig or stick. Use something that the pegs will attach to and is not too wide.

Put whatever stick you've got vertically into the dough. This is the trunk of the tree.

Now, quite simple, you build your tree, and you can be as creative as you want. The bare minimum is to try and squeeze the pegs and put them on the trunk. They look like branches on the tree. I would say these always look like trees, whatever the children do. It is impossible to not make it look like a tree!

More skilful children can build upwards by using the pegs to attach more sticks or twigs higher up. Don't worry if they can't do this – it is very much an optional extension.

A tree can be as simple or intricate as the child wants

You can jazz these trees up in multiple ways, including:

i) Have multiple branches or trunks sticking out of the dough for a wide tree (or even forest)

ii) Use different materials for leaves, blossom or fruit on the tree. Things like mini-loom bands, pieces of material, or whatever else you can find

iii) Use tiny pegs for more skilful children, or huge pegs for younger ones

iv) Take a photo of it themselves

v) Draw their tree

2. Different Theme Trees

A great way of extending this idea is to create trees at different times of the year with a specific theme.

A great example of this would be for Christmas when you can make mini-Christmas trees.

You create the same basic structure as you did before, and then decorate them with anything you can find that looks at bit Christmassy. Some examples could be:

i) Balls of play dough stuck onto loom bands to create baubles that can be placed on the ends of branches

ii) Pipe-cleaners of different sorts that look at bit like tinsel

iii) Any small baubles or pieces of tinsel you can find

iv) Children could make their own decorations and hang them on

Autumn (Fall) would be another excellent time for creating themed trees.

To create an Autumn (Fall) tree, just add some of the following:

i) Go outside and look for real fallen leaves of different colours. Try and peg them onto the trees

ii) You could use pieces of coloured paper cut up

iii) Loom bands coloured red, orange or yellow

iv) Pieces of material

Close up of some beautiful loom band blossoms on this tree!

Other types of trees could be blossom trees, fruit trees, or magical trees! The choices are endless.

3. Pirate Ships

What child doesn't love the classic theme of pirates and pirate ships!?

Clothes pins/pegs can help to create the most spectacular pirate ships, with just a few other very simple loose parts style resources.

In it's simplest form – make a pirate boat shape out of play dough. Just a long blob of dough is perfect for this.

Then use things like lolly (popsicle) sticks or twigs for the masts of the boat sticking upwards from the dough.

Onto the masts you can put pegs which look like the sails. The possibilities are then endless, and this is great to do with a full selection of loose parts objects for children to select from.

Matchsticks could be pirates.

You could make cannons, or a plank to walk from.

You could even add bottle-tops to the side and turn it into a Viking long-ship.

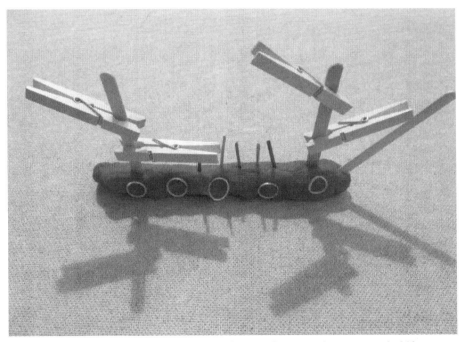

These pirates ships are amazingly engaging, and extremely open-ended if you use a range of resources for children to choose from

If the children can come up with their own ideas, that is definitely what you want. I am always happy if children deviate from the original idea in activity. If they're meant to be making pirate ships, but they make some kind of interstellar spaceship then I would say that is happy days!

However, there are lots of children that need ideas. The more you feed images and creativity into them on a daily basis, then the quicker they reach that point where they are able to unleash their own ideas on the world.

However, it definitely takes time and does not happen by chance.

4. Shark Attack!

Another extremely exciting boy-friendly idea here (though girls will like it too).

The clothes pins (pegs) are now sharks.

Get something for the sharks to eat. Something like pompoms is good for this. It's great if you have some kind of big tuff-spot or play-tray for this to keep the pompoms all in one place.

The game is very simple. One child has a peg, and they go around picking up (eating) the pompoms which are the food.

Shark attack!

There are many ways of bringing it to life, which include:

i) Use a timer. The children have a time limit (such as thirty seconds) to eat as many pieces of food as they can.

ii) You can only eat a certain colour of pompom. This is great for very young children that are learning about colours

iii) Subtraction shark attack! Have, for example, five pompoms, and the shark is going to eat three. How many will be left?

iv) Stick or draw some eyes or features on the pegs to really add that wow factor

This game is not actually as easy as it sounds, and takes a bit of resilience. A top tip is to try to keep your pegs low to the table when picking things up. This works a lot better than coming straight down on the pompoms from above. Random but true, I promise.

Children will develop their own tactics in games like this, and that is what you want. This is problem solving and critical thinking in action.

5. Different Animal Feeding Time

There are many ways that you can develop or extend the shark attack game.

One way is to have a different kind of animal (though still using a peg to represent it). Different animals will require different foods.

For example, the pegs could be eagles. You could use something like cut up pipe-cleaners for worms. (This is much trickier than pompoms just to warn you)

The pegs could be tigers, or monsters, or lions, or a T-Rex. Pretty much anything that the children are interested in, that links to a topic or theme, or is just a good fun thing to try. I would personally say that fun activities don't necessarily need to link to a theme or topic.

Some other good things to pick up with the pegs include:
    i) Cotton wool – this is easier than pompoms
    ii) Rubber bands cut up – very tricky!
    iii) Cooked spaghetti!
    iv) Material such as wool

Children can design their own pegs. This always adds to that level of ownership and involvement.

Stick things on, or jazz wooden ones up with coloured pens. They could be whatever character they like – ideally something that likes eating a lot.

8

DIY Jigsaws

Jigsaws are one of the classic fine motor activities, and in this chapter we'll take a look at some ways you can create your own.

This takes a little bit of time, but is extremely economic, and also creates lots of different opportunities that are not available with standard bought jigsaws.

Also DIY jigsaws can actually be a bit more 'fiddly' than bought, and also can provide a 'brain-teaser' in many ways.

1. Stick Jigsaws With Simple Pictures

The number one way to start with DIY jigsaws is to get some craft-sticks (lolly or popsicle sticks), and some simple pictures.

When I made them, I found some simple child-friendly images on google, copy and pasted them into word, and printed them all out in one go. I found:
   i) A horse
   ii) A boy's head
   iii) A superhero

iv) A lion

v) A rocket

But these are just examples. It really could be anything.

You could stick to a theme, for example. Maybe you print out lots of superheroes. Or you could have characters from a book the children know.

I printed out the pictures to be about six inches wide. You want two lots of the pictures – one set to make the jigsaws out of, and the other for them to refer to.

I cut them out into squares.

Then I got about ten craft-sticks, and laid them down on a table so they were next to each other, making a kind of square of craft sticks.

Then I put superglue onto the back of a picture, and laid it down on top of the sticks.

Then I repeated this for the other pictures, each on top of approximately ten sticks arranged in a row. It doesn't need to be ten, but however many that are wide enough to hold the full picture.

Wait for the superglue to dry (probably overnight), and then perform operation number two. This is to cut the picture into strips, so the individual sticks are all free to move. I used a knife for this (scissors may work).

I laminated the square pictures that were identical to the ones that I had turned into jigsaws.

And there you have it – you will have a set of DIY jigsaws.

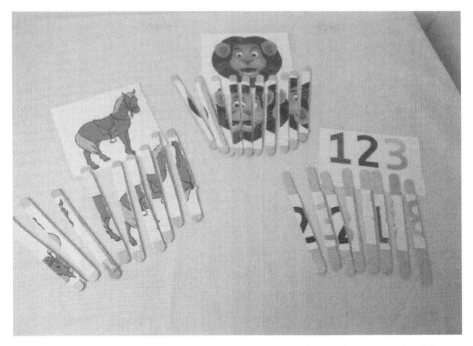

DIY jigsaws – a real brain teaser, and quite a bit more fiddly than a standard jigsaw

One nice idea is to have different coloured sticks for each jigsaw you make. So use red sticks for the lion, for example, and blue for the superhero. This helps so that the jigsaws don't get mixed up.

The idea is that a child has one full picture to look at, and the matching jigsaw to try to create.

It really does encourage pincer grip, and using fingers and thumbs to pick up the sticks and arrange them in the right place.

Also, it really does get them thinking. Because there are no grooves or connections like standard jigsaws, there is a different kind of spatial awareness involved in putting them together.

For much younger children, you can use the really wide craft sticks. You could make a jigsaw out of three or four of these together.

For older ones you could potentially make much longer jigsaws than just ten in a row. You could have the numbers in order from 0 to 10 on about 30 sticks. Just see how you get on.

2. Faces

There are many different ideas for the content of the jigsaws, but one really great suggestion is to have the children's faces for them to reassemble.

This would probably be best done on different colours again – for example, blue sticks for Imran, and yellow for Amelia. Just to stop them all getting mixed up!

Their own faces generate a lot of interest and talk in children. They could try and do their own face, or have a go of the heads of their friends.

To extend this idea, other possibilities include:
   i) The faces of adults in the setting
   ii) The faces of characters from books
   iii) The faces of characters from TV or film

3. Numbers Or Words

Of course everything should not revolve around letters and numbers, but fine motor skills can definitely be developed alongside literacy and numeracy skills.

Some ideas to incorporate this into jigsaws includes:

i) Create three letter words on the jigsaws. The children try to assemble them and sound them out. It's good if they can see the word they are trying to make somewhere else (like all these jigsaws)

ii) One-letter jigsaws. These would be good for getting them thinking about the formation of letters

iii) Sight words

iv) Ordering numbers

v) Addition sentences

vi) Single numbers (for thinking about formation)

vii) Spots or a quantity of pictures to count

viii) Some kind of pattern to re-assemble

Numbers or words could be a great option

4. Largescale Jigsaws

A beautiful thing about these jigsaws is that you can increase their size and create them with different resources.

A great way of doing it is with wooden planks of some sort. You need probably at least about 5 planks that children can handle easily – each about one or two feet long and six inches wide approximately.

Paint them with chalkboard paint. There are loads of exciting chalkboard paint activities later (so stick around for that).

Then the children can place them next to each other in a rectangle, and draw images all over them in chalk.

Mix them up, and then try to put them back together again.

They could draw pictures, or maps, or obstacle courses, or whatever else they can think of. There are a huge number of simple writing activities like this coming up in the second half of this book.

9

Tweezers Games

What a fabulous resource tweezers are for fine motor!

Great from pincer grip, squeezing, using all the muscles in your fingers, coordination, and the list goes on and on.

Also, the vast majority of educational settings will have some tweezers or tongs anyway, so with just a couple of simple resources added to the mix you will be ready to go with some scintillating fine motor experiences.

Personally I prefer the thinner tweezers you can get. Some tweezers are really wide, and the children have to use a whole-hand grasp to hold them. If you can find the thinner ones these really help for encouraging them to use fingers and thumbs.

This hand position is a great prelude for writing.

Anyway, here are some of my favourite tweezers activities:

1. Removing Seeds

This is a super simple concept.

Get some types of foods that have seeds in them, slice them open, and let the children take the seeds out with tweezers.

Some good examples of foods with seeds include:

i) Pumpkins – these have nice big seeds that are great for this activity

ii) Bell peppers – much smaller seeds that are significantly more fiddly to remove

iii) Apples – this is another quite intricate operation removing these

iv) Jackfruit – probably not available in all countries, but this is the world's largest fruit, and has spectacularly large seeds

When you have got the seeds out, you can extend this in different ways including:

i) Posting the seeds into different containers

ii) Making spells and potions

iii) Creating collages with glue

iv) Making musical shakers with plastic bottles (this would be best with larger seeds)

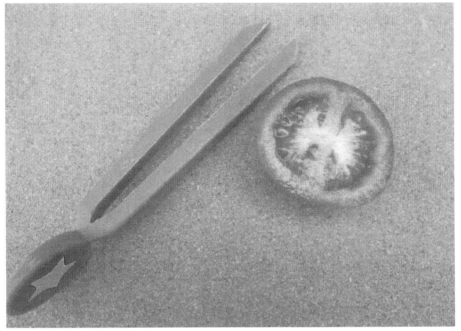

A tomato is a very tricky choice for removing seeds, great for challenging more able learners. Much easier are foods with large seeds such as pumpkins

2. Ping Pong Ball Planets

Ping pong balls are extremely cheap as long as you get the poor-quality ones. Don't be getting the world championship elite ping pong balls whatever you do.

Anyway, what you do is get some ping-pong balls and you cut the tops off. I used a knife, but I imagine scissors would probably work as well. Make sure there are no sharp spiky bits sticking out. If there are, just trim them.

Then you are going to use just a little creativity to get the ping-pong balls looking like other things.

Planets is a great one for this. There are so many children that are obsessed with space and aliens and all that kind of thing, and so tap into this natural source of enthusiasm.

To make planets, I use some acrylic paint. This type of paint basically lasts more or less forever on a range of surfaces.

Quickly paint the ping pong balls to look like different planets. Earth would be blue, with a few blobs of green for the land. Mars would be red. The sun would be yellow.

Ping pong ball planets (with a random blood-shot eyeball thrown in as well)

You can also get coloured ping-pong balls, and this would cut out this step of painting them. That would be very simple, but equally exciting.

Now you need something to fill the planets (and sun) with. Something like pompoms is perfect for this.

Holding the planets in one hand, the children will use the tweezers in their other hand to pick up pompoms and 'fill' the ping-pong ball.

If it is the earth, then you want to fill it with 'molten lava'. If it is the sun then it is 'fire', or Mars would be 'red rock'. Coloured pompoms are perfect for all these substances.

This activity takes quite a bit of coordination, as the children will require two hands to hold and synchronise - one for the ball, one for the tweezers. This is quite a bit trickier than a single-handed activity.

Also, there are many ways of extending this activity. For example, you could:

i) Have numbers on the planets. The children try to put in that many pompoms

ii) Have different themes. For example, make the ping pong balls look like eyeballs! This really taps into their grizzly sense of humour

iii) Have ping-pong balls with smaller/wider holes

For younger children, you can use a similar idea only with larger balls. Ball-pit balls would be perfect for this. Cut the tops off, and children fill them up with big pompoms. They could use tweezers or just their fingers would be fine also.

Tennis balls with the tops chopped off are another possibility.

3. Ghosts Or Snowmen

This is a beautiful and simple recycling activity.

It is also great for children that love posting things, which, to be brutally honest, is pretty much every child in history.

For this you need some recycled plastic bottles. The adult is going to chop the bottom off the bottles. Once again, I used a knife, but scissors would probably work, and watch out for those jagged bits! A bit of a trim will sort those in no time.

Now you put a face on the bottles. The adult can do this, or the children can make their own.

Two good characters to use for this are ghosts and snowmen. Some kind of very simple face is all that is required on the bottle – for example, a snowman could be two black dots drawn in permanent marker, and a triangular orange piece of card for the carrot nose:

A 'snowman' – great for any child that loves posting things (i.e. all children)

And here's a ghost:

A ghost – woo!

Then get some cotton wool balls. There are other things you can use, but these are perfect for ghosts and snowmen in particular.

Then the children fill up the bottle by posting cotton wool balls into the top. They can use tweezers to post, or just their fingers (particularly for the younger ones).

As you fill them up they become white and start to look more and more like a real ghost or snowman. Really cute!

A top tip – the children might need to hold the bottom of the bottle as they post in the top.

Some ways to further bring life to this activity include:

i) Put numbers on the ghost/snowman. It could be the number 6, and they try and post that quantity of cotton wool balls

ii) Have bottles of different sizes that they can experiment with. This is great for learning about capacity

iii) They try to fill them up against the clock

iv) The children create their own characters

v) Use bottles with really wide openings for younger children. You could even use something like tennis ball tubes

4. Birds (And Other Variations)

There are many variations of this bottles activity.

If you want to create a really challenging version, then make the bottles into birds. Some kind of simple eyes near the top of the bottle will do this, and a couple of simple wings. The bottle top is the beak of the bird.

I cut up some rubber bands when we did this. These were the worms.

The children tried to pick up the worms and post them into the bird's beak. Tricky but fun!

Another possibility is monsters filled up with something like coloured pom-poms that represent the disgusting food they love.

Of course children love pretty much anything that likes to eat a lot – lions, tigers, a T-Rex etc – so you can definitely use any of these as well. Be as creative as you want, and you could certainly link the activity to a book or theme.

5. Shot Glasses

You can buy plastic shot-glasses extremely cheaply, and they are fantastic for a range of number and fine motor experiences.

Putting numbers on them is one way to get going with multiple activities.

I like to use two separate colours, for example some green and orange shot glasses. Put some numbers on them in a way that makes a repeating pattern. For example, 1 – orange, 2 – green, 3 – orange, 4 – green, and so on.

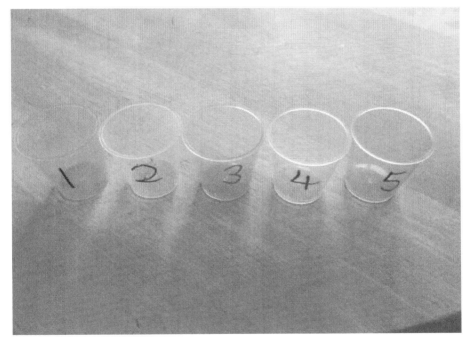

Shot glasses in a repeating pattern

Then you need something to put in them – beans, pompoms, pasta – whatever you think.

There are many games you can play. A simple one is trying to put them in order, and then fill them with the correct number of objects.

This is great for understanding how numbers get bigger. If you put the correct number of pompoms into the shot glasses, for example, you can really see the way the numbers get larger. Five looks a lot more full than one.

There are many other games you can do, such as:

i) Adding. Tip out two numbers and combine the quantity. Older children can try and record in some way

ii) Put number challenges on the shot glasses – such as '1 more than 3', or '3+2'

iii) Find shot glasses of different sizes, and put them in order of capacity

iv) Estimate how many of an object it takes to fill a shot glass

These same games can be played in other containers as well. Some good examples would be:

i) A plant-pot

ii) An egg cup

iii) An egg box

iv) Plastic pots

v) And whatever else you can find...

10

Pac-Man Monsters

This is a wonderfully random activity that I thought deserved its own mini-chapter all to itself.

This is also a blast from the past. I have a vague memory of making something similar to this when I was young.

Somehow the idea has lasted the rigour of time, and remains one of the ultimate fine motor activities that I have ever tried.

The basic idea is to get some tennis balls. I have found that cheap dog's tennis balls are best for this, as they are a bit squidgier. Proper tennis balls could be used in an emergency, but they are much firmer and more expensive.

What you do is to cut a straight line in the tennis ball. I used a knife, but probably scissors would work.

The cut will be about three inches long. This is the Pac-Man's mouth!

The idea is that you squeeze the tennis ball in your hand, and the Pac-Man mouth will open up. This is almost too exciting to behold for some children!

Also, it means many games are possible:

1. Feeding Time For Pac-Man

Definitely the number one game to start off with is 'feeding time.'

You need some kind of fake 'food' for this. Something like pompoms are the perfect choice. You could also use something like cotton wool balls or dried beans.

This game is extremely simple. It works well in some kind of big play tray, trough or tuff-spot.

Have lots of 'food' (e.g. pompoms or similar) in the tray, and the children each have a Pac-Man monster. They go around, squeezing the tennis balls, and picking up pompoms with the opening and closing mouth.

Feeding time for the Pac-Man Monsters

This is a highly addictive game, and some children will do this for literally hours.

It is great for hand strength, and even adults can really feel the muscles working and tiring in their hands after a few minutes (if you dare give it a go).

An option is to use two hands for any child that is having real problems opening the mouth – but it really is very doable with one hand for the vast majority.

Another issue is that sometimes pompoms fall out when they first get eaten. You will find that after the Pac-Man has eaten about 5 pompoms or so, this stops happening. A bit of a random top-tip for you there!

2. Time Challenge, Subtraction, Sorting

The simple way of trying the Pac-Man game is definitely the way to get going, and is so moreish that it works brilliantly.

However, you can also incorporate a range of other skills into the basic 'feeding' game.

Time challenges are great fun. In this you have some kind of sand timer – something like thirty seconds would be perfect. Turn over the timer and start 'eating'! At the end of the time the children count how many pompoms they have eaten. They can do it individually, or as a race against others.

Simple colour sorting is also possibility. There could be a Pac-Man that only eats red or green, for example. It could be signified in some way (a different coloured tennis ball, for example.)

Another game they really enjoy, though more for older children, is subtraction.

As an example, let's say you are trying to work out 5 subtract 3.

Put out 5 pompoms in a line, and then eat 3. You will be left with the correct answer as if by magic.

Pac Man subtraction – can you work out 5 subtract 3?

A really good way to make subtraction physical, visual and fun.

3. Character Tennis Balls

Another excellent way to extend this dog's ball game is to create characters.

The adult could do this beforehand, or the children could create their own.

If the adult where to create them, you could draw faces onto the balls with permanent marker, or superglue wool or other material onto them to create hair or a multi-coloured mane.

If the children are creating them, they can draw on the balls with washable pens, or stick things on with PVA glue.

A great way of bringing it to life is to really think about the characters.

Give your creation the following:
  i) A name
  ii) A funny voice
  iii) A back story

You can also link to books or topics. You could make Santa, for example, who is going to be eating 'mince pies'. Or it could be the Big Bad Wolf who is gobbling up 'pigs.'

Check out this teenage mutant ninja turtle tennis ball:

So simple to create, by just drawing straight onto the ball with pen

This element of storytelling enriches pretty much any game.

11

Fine Motor Boards

If you love a bit of DIY then you will be in your element with this one.

Alternatively, of course if you know someone else that loves DIY, this would be a great thing to try to convince them to make. They are the perfect project for caretakers, partners, brothers, sisters, dads, anyone that is wanting to help you and your children out.

The beauty of fine motor boards is that once you have made them you have them forever. It is a great investment – swap a little time and money now, and benefit by having years of high-quality learning.

Another excellent feature of them is that it is a resource you can have out pretty much all the time. It could be fixed to a wall or fence, or in a particular area, and just stay there more or less forever. They will still be used even after the children have become familiar with them.

I love evergreen resources like this partly because of the time they save in planning and preparation. Some things are just always there, *and* they work. Simple.

The basic idea of a fine motor board is that you get some kind of a surface, such as a board or plank, and then you screw lots of items to it that are great for children to fiddle with.

Here's some ideas on how to do this...

1. Creating Fine Motor Boards

There are two main ways to create fine motor boards – on a mobile surface that you can move around, or on a fixed surface (that will be there forever). The idea is basically the same for either.

To start with the mobile kind, find some kind of slab of wood that would be good for the job.

I have to admit that I didn't make any of the ones I use myself. They were made by a genius husband of a teacher I worked with at the time.

He used an offcut of a kitchen worktop, that was cut up into sections. The sections are roughly two feet by one foot (but you could definitely go bigger than this.)

Then you attach some items onto them that are great to entice children into fiddling with them, and so improving their fine motor. Some options are:
    i) An old belt
    ii) The top of a plastic bottle with it's bottle-top (that you can screw on and off)
    iii) A zip
    iv) Locks
    v) Padlocks and keys
    vi) A Lego board and some Lego pieces in a pot with a lid on to keep them in

vii) A bicycle light

viii) Baby fine motor toys – like an abacus

ix) Bolts and cogs

x) Hooks and string to weave through them

This list is pretty much the tip of the ice-berg, and there will be lots more fine motor resources you could think of.

Here are some examples of what they might look like.

Here's one with zips, light switch, handles, bolts and bottle tops:

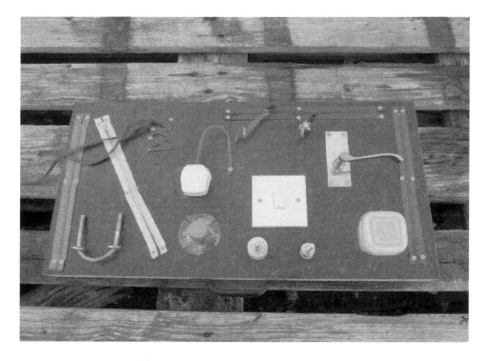

Another example is this one, with light, bolts, a baby abacus, zips, bungee cable, and a wheel:

Another one features Lego, handles, a belt, a phone charger, a wheel, a light, a zip, and a bottle-top:

And this one is a real favourite, containing plastic brackets that are great for weaving string through, as well as bolts, a light switch, a lock, a zip, a belt and a latch:

You have to be creative in how you get all these objects stuck to the board. Most you can attach by screwing them on. You could drill holes into the board for some, and attach them with cord or something similar.

Some top tips – If you have anything on the board that can come off, try to secure it in some way. For example, the keys for the padlock could be attached to the board with a string. Anything that can completely come off will do, and then will never be seen again.

Also, differentiate for the age of children you are working with. Fine motor boards for much younger children will be bigger, and have larger resources on them for smaller fingers.

2. Think Big! Largescale Fine Motor Boards

If you have the space and the capacity to do it, then going big with a fine motor board is something you will not regret.

In this way, the fine motor board will become a fixture in your setting, so a little planning is required.

Some good places to put one include:

i) On an indoor wall. Probably creating it first on a flat board, and then drilling the board to the wall is the best way around this

ii) On a fence outdoors (particularly if it has some kind of cover over it or you use things that will not rust)

iii) On an old pallet drilled to the fence (again under a cover is ideal)

iv) On the side of a cupboard

v) On the side of a shed

These largescale boards are great for all sorts of substantial locks, bolts, padlocks, and any other mechanisms you can find that are basically BIG.

Check out this one made out of a wooden frame and an assortment of locks and handles:

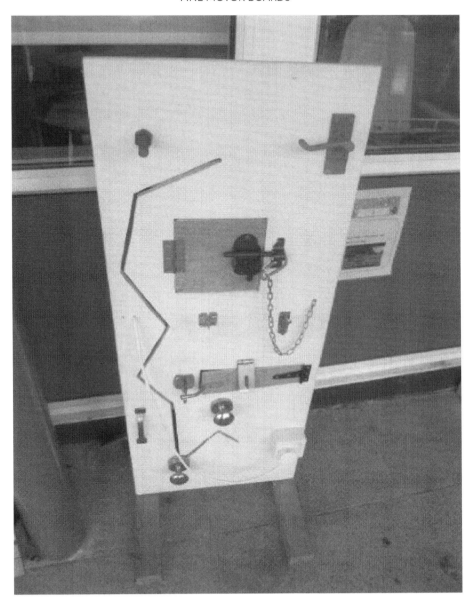

The same DIY legend that made the fine motor boards, also created this spectacular ball wall which was brilliant for problem solving and fine motor:

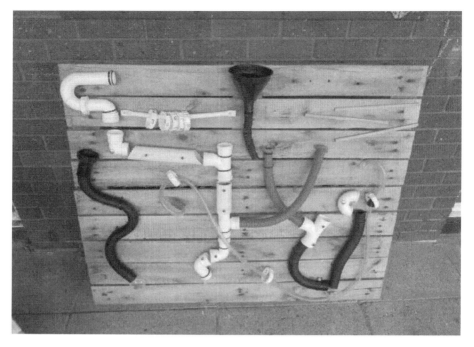

A ball wall

It's called a 'ball-wall' because you roll small balls down the tubes. The tubes can all be fiddled with, and you can change the direction that the balls will roll. Fantastic for problem solving, critical thinking, and fine motor control, all in one mighty fine cocktail.

3. Easels Fine Motor Boards

I saw one of these in a school recently, and it was such a simple and excellent idea that I've included it here.

They had basically found an old triangular art easel, and had drilled lots of fine motor experiences all over both sides of it.

This creates a brilliant experience at the child's height, and also the chance for several children to interact with it whilst standing around the board at the same time.

Final Thoughts

And so we come to the end of the first part of this book.

I hope you now have a treasure trove of exciting activities and provocations to try out, and get all children (or at least the vast majority) interested and engaged.

As a surprise gift, there is lots of extra fine motor content that you can find on my website at this page – https://earlyimpactbooks.com/bonus/

This includes:

-5 Bonus Genius Fine Motor Activities (not found in this book)

-101 Fine Motor/Early Writing Activities Cheat Sheet

-A free fine motor video – Magical Fine Motor Pipettes Ideas!

But, don't go anywhere just yet, as we are only halfway through our journey.

Next we're going to dive into some really juicy early writing ideas, that hopefully will bridge the gap between children making marks for the first time, and later writing letters and words.

II

Early Writing Activities

12

Early Writing

Learning to write is a huge process that takes many years. There are distinct stages that children go through, and there are many strategies to help them on the way.

This book focuses on one of the major stages of this process.

It charts the time in between children first making marks in different ways, all the way through a long journey to the end-point where they are able to begin writing letters.

This really is the engine room of the whole process of writing. Get this right and children will be well equipped both physically and *emotionally* to start writing letters, words and sentences.

Why physically? Because they will have learned to coordinate their movements, developed their fine motor, and have a proficient level of hand-eye coordination required to begin.

That is much more obvious.

But how do I mean *emotionally* ready you might ask?

The biggest thing to instill in children is the desire to make marks. If they want to write, then writing will happen.

If you lure children in through a series of engaging and exciting activities over a long time-span, this is much more likely to be the case. It's not one hundred per cent guaranteed for all children, of course, but the odds do go up a lot in your favour.

We will look at how to create the bridge across these two distinct points in time – from starting out to writing letters.

It's a big process!

Just to recap some of the most important themes of this book, first let's take a look at some top tips, and how to apply them to early writing:

1. Think About The Boys

This is not sexism, I promise you!

However, I would say that if you can motivate the boys, then pretty much everyone will be engaged. I know this is a generalisation, but I think this is roughly the reality of things.

Unmotivated and uninterested boys will lead to many girls following suit, and the whole provision breaking down into boredom.

Excite the boys, and the girls will be excited as well.

Go boy-heavy on topics and themes for success in early writing. Think dinosaurs, vehicles, superheroes, and all that kind of thing.

2. Make Everything Compelling

The initial 'hook' is crucial.

Storytelling and imagination is important for many activities. It provides a backdrop and a way-in.

Think excitement, curiosity, fireworks!

3. Keep Things Simple And Open

You don't need a whole load of intricate resources. Pretty much everything we'll look at is either extremely cheap or free.

Just a little bit of imagination can really bring these simple things to life.

Open-ended is also important. Although I do think a bit of structure is crucial in getting children used to resources and how to use them, once they are familiar most of these things can be used in multiple ways.

An Important Tool Of The Trade

The other major thing to know about is a key tool at our disposal.

This tool is called 'writing patterns', and it is central to development throughout this phase. If you're not sure what writing patterns are, then you're about to find out...

13

Writing Patterns

Writing patterns are known by several different names. They are also called 'pre-writing patterns' (particularly in the US). They are also sometimes referred to as 'handwriting patterns'. I have also heard them called mark-making patterns.

All these things are roughly the same thing.

Writing patterns are simple types of lines that are excellent for children to try to create.

Examples are things like circles and a line of dots.

Examples of writing patterns on these beautiful stones

Writing patterns could also be zig-zags, swirls, waves on the sea, horizontal lines, and any other type of simple structured marks such as this.

These patterns have multiple benefits for getting children engaged in early writing. Let's take a look at some of them now...

The Benefits Of Writing Patterns

Structure

Writing patterns help children to get a level of structure into their early writing.

Patterns encourage them to begin moving mark-making tools in different directions and in different formations.

Seeing writing patterns modelled provides images and a template in their minds. It gives them a guide.

Everyone needs structure of some sort to begin to write. However free and open-ended and child-centred your provision is, early writing will not flow out of this without some level of *structure*.

Big Or Small Scale

One of the beauties of writing patterns is that they can be done both on a small and a big scale.

This is good news, because at this early stage children are developing both their fine motor and their gross motor at the same time, and there is a massive link between the two.

Writing patterns can be done in the air, or with paint brushes on fences, or with all sorts of other large equipment.

They help develop movements in their core, arms, shoulders and wrists, as well as helping them coordinate fine motor skills in their fingers and hands.

Introduce Different Movements

Trying to copy writing patterns gets children's arms and hands moving in ways they will not have experienced before.

These patterns will introduce some of the following movements:
   -Writing horizontally

-Writing vertically
-Going anticlockwise
-Writing clockwise
-Creating curves and loops
-Creating straight lines
-Creating circles and other shapes

All of these many and varied directions and movements can be done in different contexts. For example they could:
-Be done on a big scale or small
-Be done in a range of exciting and fun ways
-Use loose parts and other objects

Are Achievable

Writing patterns can be extremely simple. This is great as children are able to do them!

This boosts their confidence and self esteem. Early success is crucial with writing activities.

There is an order to follow where writing patterns are concerned. They start really easy, but can grow increasingly more complex (if required). More about the order I think it's a good idea to use in a few moments.

When To Use Them

Writing patterns are the phase of writing in between very early mark-making (i.e. 'scribbles' and dots), and later on using letters.

The time to use them is basically all the way between these two points. This can be quite a long period (many months or years), and is dependent on the child.

Start to use them when a child has become confident at making simple marks. These will often look like a 'scribbly' line, circles or dots.

Introducing writing patterns in a fun, enticing, and active way will give you a much higher likelihood of success.

The Main Writing Patterns – The Order

OK, this bit is crucial.

There is an order from easier to harder. This is not set in stone, but I would say that it looks something like this:

Step 1 – Circles And Dots

This is what many children start with anyway in their early writing, so it is good to follow the order of nature.

Dots can go in different directions – e.g. horizontal or vertical.

The same with circles – they can be drawn in a line in different directions.

Circles and dots can be big or small!

Step 2 – Straight Lines

The simplest straight lines to try are vertical or horizontal.

However, you can definitely expand to diagonal lines as well.

Once again, you can model these kinds of lines in a sequence, such as a line of vertical lines, or a line of horizontal lines.

Step 3 – Curved and Changing Lines

The most common of these are:

Zig-zags – These are normally quite achievable for most children.

Waves on the sea – A wiggly line that can be shallow or more pronounced.

Springs – These are more difficult and really expand their spatial awareness. It is a continually curving line that interlocks over itself.

Crosses – Another very achievable one. Great for treasure maps – and x marking the spot.

Zig-zags, waves, crosses and springs

Step 4 – More Complex Lines

Turrets on a castle – These require quite a bit more spatial awareness, and moving in straight lines in several different directions.

Spirals – These look a bit like a snail shell.

Complex wave patterns – These look like lifelike waves. They are great for beginning to form simple handwriting movements.

Turrets on a castle, a spiral, and a more complex 'waves on the sea' pattern

Step 5 – Some Simple Letters

You can definitely incorporate some letters into writing patterns later on. Particularly the simpler ones to write are best for this.

This is letters like 'o', 'i', and 'l'.

What Next?

OK, so now you know all about writing patterns. But the next big question is how to get children started.

A top tip is not to just throw a load of writing patterns into the situations they are playing in, and hope for the best. The chances of this leading to much are extremely low.

Writing patterns will take at least a little adult interaction to get them started, and then lots of modelling of how to use them in fun situations.

14

Introducing Writing Patterns

I would say the number one way to introduce writing patterns is through skywriting.

This is an adult-led activity, and I just think it needs this initial push to get children understanding what writing patterns are before they really try them out with writing tools.

Like anything, the key is to make it fun and exciting!

That's why I use superhero lasers, pumping music – the full works!

In a nutshell, 'skywriting' is pretending to make big writing pattern movements in the air. You could use your finger to draw big lines, or use one of the several strategies we're about to have a look at.

Skywriting is really multi-sensory. Children will be responding to sound and sight, whilst using their whole bodies to move. This is a definite formula for high-quality learning.

1. Skywriting With Torches

This is my number one sky-writing trick.

You require one mini-torch per child. They are going to hold this in their hand, turned on and pointing away from them.

The torch is going to be the 'superhero laser'! This just really brings it to life that little bit more.

Humble torches are transformed into 'superhero lasers'

This can be done as a simple group activity, with all children facing an adult.

If you are able to dim the lights then go for it. The darker the better for extra excitement. However, if this is virtually impossible for you, never fear! Skywriting in the light is still exciting as well.

Standing up is better than sitting down, as you can then move your whole bodies, stretching as high as you can, and down to the ground as required.

I like to put some music on for skywriting.

Anything with a good, pumping beat is perfect. I like to use music without any words if you can find it.

Then you, the adult, will start doing some writing patterns in the air to the music.

For example, do dots to the beat of the music, with your torch making the dot.

The children will hopefully copy.

Then try other patterns, such as vertical lines.

I always go from right to left when I am modelling the lines. Hopefully the children will copy this movement, but they will do so like a mirror. If you go right to left, then they will go left to right. I hope this makes sense!

You want them to go from left to right in the movements because this begins the process of moving in this direction when they write later on.

Instilling this left to right movement in big action-packed skywriting will at least start this process, which can be built on in later activities.

Remember the order of writing patterns to follow – start easy with dots and lines, and potentially extend to circles, zigzags and all that kind of thing. You can see how the children are doing as you go, and just keep making it that tiny little bit harder step by step.

This activity is also great in the following ways:

i) If you can get it quite dark, then you can all draw patterns on the wall or ceiling

ii) You can do it inside a dark den

iii) You can use the torches to draw over large writing patterns that you could draw on big paper and attach to the wall or under a table

2. Ribbons, Streamers, Fingers

You can use the same skywriting process, but instead of using little torches, there are all sorts of exciting things you can use:

i) *Streamers* – You can buy many different types of children's streamers that work really well for skywriting

ii) *Ribbons* – Simply cut up a longer piece of ribbon into smaller sections about one foot long. These work great for twirling and creating different movements

iii) *Cheerleader pompoms* – I've never tried these but I don't see why they wouldn't work!

iv) *Fingers* – This is a simple but effective way of doing skywriting. You can also draw patterns on different things using fingers. You can draw them on your hand, on your friend's back, on your leg, on the floor, in mud, or wherever else.

3. Big Surface Write

This is kind of the next step on from skywriting, but it's a very similar process.

For this you need some kind of huge surface. Wallpaper on the floor would be good, and you can mark-make on it with pens.

Alternatively, something like chalks on the concrete floor would also work well.

Once again music works really well for this, so put some on if you can. If you are outside this might be trickier, so it is not essential.

The adult is going to start making some writing patterns on the surface, moving to the music if you're using it. The children are going to try to copy.

Keep going, trying out whatever range of patterns you are up to.

Some ways of bringing this to life even more include:
   i) Experiment with the children using both hands to write with
   ii) Make fun noises and sounds as you do it! The dots could be exploding, or the spirals like fireworks!

15

Early Writing Dice And Stones

In the last chapter we explored some excellent adult-led strategies to start children off with writing patterns, but the remainder of this book will be activities that are more child-led and that can be done completely independently as well.

Two beautiful resources that we are going to look at in this chapter are writing stones, and early writing dice.

Both are cheap, and relatively simple to create. The added beauty is that once made they will pretty much last a lifetime.

1. Early Writing Dice

You can make writing dice in different ways.

A great way is using wooden cubes. You could use some wooden building blocks, for example.

I have also made writing dice before out of an old fence post that I sawed up into cubes (and sanded down quickly to prevent any splinters).

Whatever type of cube you use, the idea is that you draw simple writing patterns or marks on the dice. For example, you might have a dice with zigzags on one side, dots on another, a spiral on another, and so on.

A beautiful way to try this activity that really brings it to life is to have a theme.

Some of the ultimate themes that I have tried that they really enjoyed are the following:

A pizza topping dice! – This is probably the number one dice that I have ever used. It simply has a different pizza topping on each face. For example, there are round dots for olives, three lines for bacon, wavy lines for peppers, a mushroom shape for the mushrooms, and so on.

The delicious pizza topping dice - yum!

A seaside dice – This has lines on such as wavy lines for the sea, simple fish, jellyfish, seaweed, and other simple representations

The seaside dice

A space dice – These are brilliant for all the space enthusiasts, and there are always lots of them where young children are concerned. Good marks include: circles for moons, dots for stars, crescent moons, whooshing vertical lines for rockets, and whatever else you can think of.

Simple stars and moons on the space dice

Pick one of these dice, or something similar, and then I think it works well to use it as part of a challenge.

For example, if you are going to use the pizza dice, announce that you are going to all create 'the biggest pizza in the world'. Get the children to create a massive pizza shape on the ground – you could use chalks on the concrete, or pens on huge wallpaper.

Then someone rolls the dice, and everyone adds the 'topping' to the pizza. For example, if you throw olives, then everyone draws small dots all over it. If they roll tomatoes, they draw circles.

Keep rolling and drawing until you have the world's biggest pizza!

If you use the space dice, then you are creating the world's biggest space-map on the floor. The aliens will be able to see it from space, and come to visit.

If you use the seaside dice, you are making a giant seaside picture on the ground.

Whatever the theme, I think some kind of challenge like this will fire up the children's imagination. If they can think of their own challenge idea then amazing! That is the ultimate goal. But many children will have to be fed lots of ideas over a long period before they start to produce their own inventions.

Other types of dice you could use for this include the large foam ones that have pockets in. Create writing patterns on paper and slip them into the pockets.

I have also heard recently that you can buy whiteboard dice, that have six whiteboard faces that you can write on with washable pen. These would be amazing if you can get hold of any.

2. Dice Linked To Books

A great way to use these dice is linked to a book that the children know well.

If you can think of some patterns or marks that link well to the illustrations then you are definitely onto a winner.

Some examples are:
   i) *Harold and The Purple Crayon* – The boy in this book creates his own reality by simple images that he draws with a purple crayon that come to life
   ii) *The Very Hungry Caterpillar* – Draw some of the simplest foods on the dice
   iii) *Triangle*, by Mac Burnett – This is a fantastic book that contains different triangles and squares, all of which could be put onto a separate side of the dice

(with a few other shapes maybe thrown in)

'Triangle' by Mac Barnett and Jon Klassen contains lots of fantastic 2D shapes that are great to put on a dice

3. Abstract Dice

Although I have found better results in the past by using a dice with a theme, this is certainly not compulsory. Many educators prefer to keep things as open-ended as possible, and you can achieve this by using an abstract dice.

You create a similar dice as before, but this time it will just have simple abstract writing patterns on it – for example, zig-zags, dots, lines, dots, squiggles, waves on the sea, and all that kind of thing.

You roll the dice and try to copy the patterns. This process can be extended in many ways, such as:

i) Children try to invent their own meanings in the symbols. For example, dots could be magic dust, or a terrible skin disease

ii) Draw or write in different exciting substances with unusual materials – for example, with sticks in the mud, or using their fingers in a tray of glitter

iii) Create their own challenges based on the symbols they find on the dice (this is quite a bit harder)

4. Writing Pattern Stones

If you want the ultimate open-ended writing pattern resource, then these beautiful writing pattern stones could be just the very thing.

They are so simple to make. Find or buy some pebbles and put some writing patterns on them.

I have used differently coloured stones over the years, and currently I am using some spectacular white and sparkly stones. They are really good for contrasting brilliantly with the black lines.

Put all sorts of simple marks over whatever stones you find – circles, dots, zig-zags, spirals, and all that kind of thing.

Sparkly, magical writing pattern stones

You can use them in all the same ways as you used the abstract dice in the activity above.

However, my number one way of using them is to create stories.

This is best done in an adult-led context, at least to start with.

Have a group of children sit in a circle around a big surface that they are going to draw and write on. It could be around a huge piece of wallpaper, for example, or they could be using chalks on the ground.

Have the stones in a box or bag. Take out the first stone.

It could be, for example, some dots. Make up a story. If the children can make it up themselves, then that is fantastic! That is exactly what you want.

However, if they can't then it is no problem – you just make it up for them.

Either way, they are going to be doing lots of drawing and marks throughout the story.

It might go something like this: (Take out the dots stone) 'One day Amelia found some magic dust.'

Everyone does lots of dots all over the surface to signify the magic dust.

(Take out the stone with triangles on it). 'She took it to the mountains.'

The children draw lots of triangle mountains.

(Next is the stone with zig-zags on it). 'Suddenly a giant T-Rex jumped out on her and showed its white teeth!'

Keep going like this, making up a story, and all making the same marks together. The storytelling element really helps in getting them engaged, and wanting to do it.

Storytelling combined with simple pattern writing using the abstract story stones

I find that if I do an activity like this a few times with a group of children, their confidence grows a lot and some will start helping with the storytelling element.

16

Secret Missions

If there is one thing that guarantees a level of true excitement in young children, then it is secrecy!

Anything that involves top-secret missions, or spies, detectives, undercover agents or invisible superheroes is truly guaranteed to fire up their curiosity like pretty much nothing else.

But how can you include secret missions in early writing?

The answer is in many, many ways, and just to prove it here are some of the best.

1. Spy Pens

These are one of the greatest and simplest purchases you can ever make.

Google 'invisible ink pens' and you should see the kind of thing I'm talking about.

They are pens that you buy that write in ultra-violet ink. They look a bit like this:

'Spy pens' – (commonly known as 'invisible ink pens' to the wider world)

I always call them 'spy pens' with the children. They write in invisible ink, but they have an ultra-violet torch in the top of the lid. The children make some marks and then shine the torches over what they have written. Hey presto – the secret code emerges.

These pens are brilliant for a range of activities.

They are a fantastic way of engaging children that are simply not interested in writing. Hopefully if you've got a top-secret spy pen then it's a completely different story!

Some tips to make the process even more exciting:

i) Stick pieces of paper in all sorts of unusual places for them to write 'code' on. Under a table is a good one. In a dark den. Maybe under a chair, or on the side of a cupboard. Anywhere dark and out of the ordinary is perfect

ii) Have little 'clue-cards' stuck on the wall all round the room. The children can either write or read the 'clues' (any kind of marks will work!)

iii) Make the pens a special event. They could come wrapped in paper, or from inside a treasure chest.

iv) Send them from space! The alien's have sent them to turn us into amazing secret writers

v) Don't have them out all the time! They will get wrecked after a few weeks. They are more of a special event, and I think should be used sparingly.

A top secret spy-pen in action

For older children, you can also use these pens to create number or phonics trails around the room.

Create small cards with symbols on, and the children go around the room, find out what's written on them, and either try and read it, or also write something as well.

Some ideas include:

i) Number or letter recognition – read the letter or number, and then write your own secret one on the card

ii) Read three letter words, sight words, or simple captions

iii) Answer phonic questions, such as 'Is the moon green?' Children write a tick or a cross

iv) Number problems, such as addition, subtraction, or finding one more or less

A word of warning is that most of the pens you buy will be for children aged 3 or upwards. I don't believe they are particularly toxic, but you don't want to be sucking on one for a very long time, and stick to the age suggested.

2. Torch Pens

These are kind of like a DIY version of the spy pens.

They are very simple to construct. All you need is some kind of small torch and a pen, and you simply tape one to the other so that the light is shining in the same direction as the pen. Any kind of tape will work well – Sellotape, for example, would be perfect.

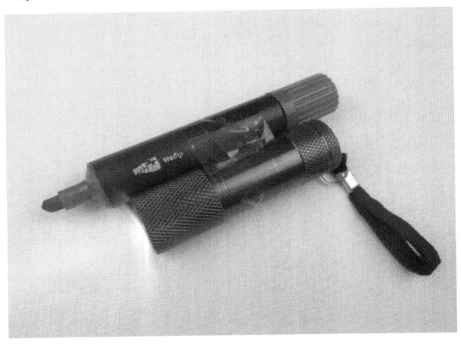

What do you get when you tape a torch to a pen? A 'top-secret torch pen' of course

These are strongly targeted at reluctant children again. They may hate writing or any kind of making marks – but hopefully that's all before they test out the top-secret torch pen.

These pens are great for making all sorts of 'code' in secret places. Any kind of dark den would be perfect. This could be:
   i) Created by either the adults or children
   ii) Be made out of a sheet over a table, or a shelf
   iii) Be the inside of a large box

3. Secret Code

Now on to secret code itself.

This is many activities in one, and you really can be as creative as you like.

The basic idea is to have pieces of card or paper that contain the 'code'. Secret code is basically writing patterns! Think dots, squiggles, zigzags, and all that sort of thing.

Top secret code

It's good to have 'code' on display that the children can copy. Also they'll need a range of materials to put the code on – things like pieces of card, paper, cards, envelopes, and anything else like that.

Some exciting writing tools would be good as well – pencils with superhero pictures stuck on, pens with torches on them, or anything else like that.

One simple thing that brings code-writing to life is 'posting'. Having secret boxes with slits in, or strange chests, or anything that can be used to post the code into really helps.

I once used some plastic cups that I cut a slit into the top of. These were great for posting tiny messages.

You could jazz up a cardboard box in some way. For example, a box with a superhero on it can represent the secret headquarters.

They also like boxes with animals on like sharks, and you can feed the code to the sharks.

It all sounds ridiculous, but really addictive for some children!

4. Copying Lines And Markings

All you need is a little imagination for this, and it is great for all the lovers of missions and 'codes.'

It is best done outside this idea.

Basically you find some kind of marks in the environment and try to draw over them or copy them.

An example could be a wall. Draw with chalks over the lines that run in between the bricks. This is creating secret code!

Other lines and markings that are worth checking out include:
  i) Playground markings – either draw over them or next to them
  ii) Any strange markings near drains or on walls
  iii) Any lines on the floor
  iv) Drawing on fences

You can draw 'code' pretty much anywhere, and by just creating an imaginary web of secrecy it brings it all to life in an extraordinary way for many.

You can also draw 'clues' all over the place as well. A squiggle on the floor could have all sorts of exciting meanings associated with it.

17

Chalkboard Paint

Pretty much all you need for the activities in this chapter is a trusty tin of chalkboard paint.

I find this a magical substance, that can help you bring early writing into all sorts of play situations and scenarios. You simply paint different surfaces with it, and the children can then mark-make on them with chalks (and rub it off when they've finished.)

The classic chalkboard paint is black, but these days you can get a variety of different colours.

I always feel a bit like Willy Wonka when using chalkboard paint. I have experimented with many strange objects and surfaces, and it is a fantastic vent for creativity.

Through experimenting, I have found that you can paint pretty much any surface. Of course wood is fantastic, and most wooden surfaces such as fences, tables and sheds only require one coat of chalkboard paint and they are ready to go.

However, a revelation I found is that you can paint many other materials as well. These appear to include plastic and metal. You just seem to need two coats if you paint these things. If you use just one coat, the paint will scrape off. But two coats, and it stays on for a considerable length of time.

What, then, are the best things to cover with chalkboard paint? Although your imagination can know no bounds, here are some scintillating ideas to get you started:

1. Wooden Bricks In A Block Area

This is a beautiful and open-ended way of exploring mark-making on chalkboard paint.

Select a few blocks from your block area to paint. Don't do them all if you have hundreds! I would pick maybe about ten, though you could do a few more. It's nice to have a bit of variation in size and shape of block. One coat of paint is normally all that is needed.

That's pretty much all you have to do.

You then keep some chalks always in the area, and do plenty of modelling to show the children how you can draw and write on the blocks (just the ones with the paint on!)

The beauty of this is that the blocks can represent so many things in the children's play and building activities. For example, they could be:

i) Characters – with just a few lines the blocks could become goodies, baddies, superheroes, dinosaurs – whatever they imagine

ii) Buildings – It's very simple to add windows, doors and other features

iii) Vehicles – Think superhero vehicles, spaceships, racing cars, monster trucks, and all that kind of thing

iv) Anything else the children can think up

The blocks can be transported round the area, or used to build with, or feature in a kind of small-world play meets construction environment. Fabulously open-ended which is great for learning across the whole curriculum.

If you do no other chalkboard paint activity, please do this one!

2. Animals With Natural Patterns On Their Skins

It was trying this that I made the revelatory discovery that you can paint onto plastic.

Animals that have natural patterns on their skins are brilliant for all sorts of writing shapes and lines. What you do is find some kind of unwanted plastic animal toys and paint them with chalkboard paint. Two coats is the way to go with these and any other plastic items. Paint them once, let the objects to dry, and then paint them again.

Some brilliant animals to use for this if you can find them include:
i) Animals with stripes – zebras, tigers, chipmunks, cats
ii) Giraffes – with that beautiful segmented pattern they have that you can try to copy with squares or circles

A painted giraffe provides a beautiful canvas for creating simple patterns

iii) Anything with spots – leopards, cheetahs, or jaguars

A cheetah prowling in the undergrowth, ready to have spots drawn all over it

iv) Animals with scales such as fish – you can try to create these with a repeating 'u' shape

Fish are fantastic for trying out the repeated 'u' scale pattern

It's good for the children to be able to see pictures of what these animal skins look like in reality, to give them a fighting chance of being able to replicate it.

The children can use all sorts of colours and create really psychedelic animals!

Lots of exciting writing pattern experimenting, but with a purpose!

3. Play-Items

There are so many objects that children play with on a daily basis that you could paint with chalkboard paint as a way of encouraging early writing in an organic context.

A few ideas that I have tried include...

i) A globe – This required two coats of paint. The globe in question I found very cheaply in a charity shop. It was used prolifically over several years. The globe was brilliant for pirate role-play. You could draw treasure maps on it, for example. It was also good for maps of the earth, and older children could write the names of cities and countries on it. Great for mark-making as part of role-play.

A globe – fantastic for pirate role-play

ii) A castle – I painted a few plastic objects that were getting thrown out of our sand area, and the real winner was a plastic castle (the type for making sand-castles). Painted with black chalkboard paint it became a haunted castle. Great for drawing on ghosts, skeletons, knights, Rapunzel in the tower, and other things like that. You could also trace round the windows and bricks.

An old bucket from the sandpit is given a new lease of life with a coat of chalkboard paint

iii) Plates – These can then be used for a variety of purposes. They are great in a role-play area. You can draw food onto them. They could also be good for learning about healthy eating. Or you could draw alien or monster food onto them.

iv) A doll's house – This is another really open-ended activity. The doll's house can take on many different roles when painted. It could become a haunted castle, Hansel and Gretel's Cottage, the princess palace – the potential is huge

4. Large Wooden Surfaces

Thinking 'big' is definitely the way to go with chalkboard paint.

Large surfaces allow a huge amount of gross motor development to happen alongside fine motor. Children will be developing coordination in their wrists, arms, shoulders and core.

Also big equals exciting!

I think the best outdoor chalkboard experiences are mostly going to be large. Some examples of things to paint are:

i) Sheds – it may just be part of a shed, such as one wall, or just a section of one surface. Or you can do the whole thing!

ii) Part of a fence

iii) Tables and chairs – when I tried this, the children found mark-making on the chair much more exciting than the table. I think this had to do with an element of 'danger'! Giving them things to write on that they know are definitely normally out of bounds adds a real allure to the process. With regards to tables, painting the underneath of them makes this very exciting.

iv) Planks of wood

v) A pallet

vi) Cable reels

vii) Wood slices

This wood slice covered in chalkboard paint becomes a fantastic surface for exploring writing patterns and loose parts

5. Things They Are Interested In

Returning to this question is crucial in mark-making – what are they interested in?

Find the things they like, and experiment with covering a few of them in chalkboard paint.

Some classic ideas would be things like:
   i) Vehicles
   ii) Dinosaurs
   iii) Superheroes

iv) Animals

Of course you will have children that are interested in other things as well, and just give whatever it is a go.

Whenever you have a clear-out of your school or nursery, be on the lookout for any objects that could be painted on.

6. Random Objects

A few more ideas to finish this chapter with now.

Random objects are usually pretty plentiful when you work with young children! Some of these might be perfect for being plastered with chalkboard paint. Some suggestions are:

i) That odd Wellington boot that always seems to end up lying about for a few months and is unclaimed. Great for designing with all sorts of mark-making lines

ii) Rubber balls of different sizes – great for creating the solar system, or designing alien planets

iii) Stones – children can write numbers or pictures on

18

Wrapping Paper

Birthdays are one of the most exciting things known to man if you are a young child. If you're 3 or 4 or 5, you have to talk about it all day!

Everyone has to go around chatting about the day, about the party, and giving each other fake presents such as play dough cakes.

Luckily, we get to tap into all this wonderful enthusiasm, and use it as a source of endless early writing.

But how do we capture this opportunity?

Through the medium of wrapping paper!

There are many ways of doing this, as we shall shortly see. However, the basic idea is that you are going to make some kind of fake presents for the lucky person whose birthday it is, but the big emphasis is going to be in creating the finest wrapping paper imaginable to wrap them up with.

Here are some ways of doing it:

1. Making Wrapping Paper

This is the key game, and the one to start out with.

It is good planned in advance. Find out when some of the children's birthdays are that you work with, and pick the nearest one coming up.

This is the lucky person who is going to get the wrapping paper experience first in all its glory.

Get some big paper, and something like brightly coloured pens is great for the mark-making side.

It is good to give them some visual ideas for different patterns they can make on the wrapping paper.

I like to make an 'ideas card'. This is really easy – you basically get a piece of card folded in half with some writing patterns on it, and stand it up on the table for them to see. You could also make a really big ideas sheet on the wall to look at.

A small-scale 'ideas card', but you could also make much larger ones and stick them on the wall

All the standard writing patterns like dots, zig-zags, spirals and all the rest of it would be perfect.

Then the children go to work designing magical wrapping paper.

Creating wrapping paper using an ideas card for the lucky birthday boy or girl

It really is an activity to get your more reluctant mark-makers on board. Who can resist the allure of birthdays?

When you've made plenty of wrapping paper, you can then go on to make presents of some description. These could be:

i) Artworks

ii) Models made from recycled boxes

iii) Collages

Basically anything that the children make, but not using resources that you need to keep in the room. Once wrapped up, you will never see them again!

After doing this in a more adult-led way the first time you try it, it could become a more child-led activity in the future, when the next lucky person on the list reaches a magical milestone.

2. Bought Patterned Wrapping Paper

This is another way of creating the wrapping paper, that taps into the same basic structure as the last game.

In this way of doing it, instead of using blank paper for the wrapping paper, you instead use real wrapping paper that you either buy or is donated to you.

You are looking for wrapping paper with some kind of patterns or lines on it, for example with:

i) Zig-zag patterns

ii) Dots

iii) Circles

iv) Squiggly lines

v) Shapes

vi) Repeating simple pictures

Basically anything you can find that has been manufactured with simple mark-making lines all over it.

The activity is simple – the children are going to use pens, crayons or pencils to draw directly onto this wrapping paper.

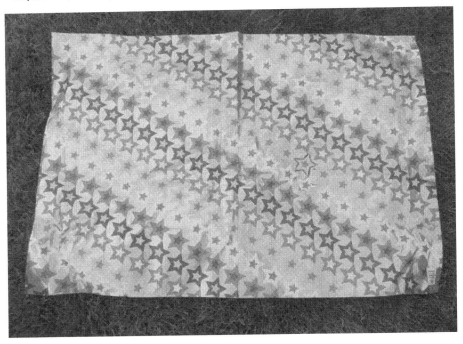

Some kind of patterned wrapping paper is all you need

It is kind of like a fun tracing activity. They follow the lines and shapes with their pens or crayons, drawing over the top of what is already there.

A top tip - some pens don't work well on glossy wrapping paper, but crayons seem to work on everything.

3. Santa's Elves In The Grotto

Alongside birthdays, what else could be more exciting than Christmas?

This also gives us the opportunity to adapt this enjoyment of creating wrapping paper, and lending it a Christmas theme.

The idea now is that the children are going to be elves in the grotto, and they are going to be churning out wrapping paper for Santa.

This has the added attraction that whereas before you were only making wrapping paper for that specific person whose birthday it was, now you can make it for anyone – your mum, your best friend, your teacher, and anyone else you might want to consider. Wrapping paper can be mass-produced like never before.

The practicalities of doing the activity are basically the same as before. Just get paper, pens, and some kind of ideas card to copy from, as this really helps them to get structure and confidence into their marks.

Other potential options are:
   i) Using paint in some way to create the paper – painting lines or printing
   ii) Drawing over Christmas paper
   iii) Using things like glitter pens to make it look really Christmassy, if you don't mind the mess

4. Wrapping Random Things Up And Decorating Them

This one is really quite bizarre, but just something that young children like to do.

Have some large sheets of paper and masking tape.

The children find things around the room to wrap up. Quite small things are best. They can use anything this time, as long as the things are not fragile. You will be getting them back at the end of the experience, so don't worry about not seeing them again.

Some good things to wrap up might be:
  i) A toy vehicle
  ii) A cuddly toy or puppet
  iii) A book
  iv) Wooden blocks

The children wrap up their selected thing in paper, and tape it shut with masking tape. The wrapping up doesn't have to look perfect! (And it definitely won't)

Now they are going to draw on the paper, re-designing the object.

For example, if it is puppet, they can draw a face on and give it an expression. They could change the face, or give the puppet clothes. They can basically be as imaginative as they want.

For something really open-ended, like a wooden block, they could draw marks on it that transforms it into something else. It could be a vehicle, or a building, or a character.

It sounds crazy this activity, but they really enjoy it!

19

Obstacle Courses And Maps

Children love to be on a quest.

They like to pretend they are superheroes, or that they are on missions. They love thinking that they are on a magical adventure, or searching for hidden treasure.

This sense of adventure and quest is captured by creating obstacle courses and maps.

These are best done outside, with lots of found objects, such as stones, sticks, and whatever else.

Here are some ideas to try:

1. Simple Obstacle Courses

There are all sorts of ways to do these.

You basically get some kind of big surface, like paper or concrete, and create an obstacle course out of lots of random objects. Outside it could be things like stones or leaves.

Then you get a pen or chalk, and try to draw around the obstacles without touching them.

An element of story added to the obstacles really helps.

For example, this was the moon's craters, and the astronauts were trying to travel around them without falling in:

A few simple curtain hooks on the ground...or is it craters on the moon's surface?

You could have lots of sticks all over the place, as another example, and these are the trees in the haunted forest. Make your path around the trees, so you don't run in to any evil spirits.

2. Vehicle Obstacle Courses

I have found that this obstacle course activity gets really super-charged if there are vehicles involved.

It can be something as simple as drawing around a group of cars placed randomly around a big piece of paper. These could be cars in the car-park.

Another simpler way to incorporate vehicles, is to drive them around the obstacles in the course. So, for example, have lots of nuts and leaves all over the floor outside, and the cars drive in and out in between them, being careful not to touch the obstacles.

Although there is no actual marks being made in this, there are similar skills involved. It still requires coordination, and the ability to move the vehicle along different lines.

3. Making Maps

This is another really open-ended activity, that can be linked to a quest or a mission.

Once again, it is good on a big outdoor surface.

You are basically going to end up with a map on the floor.

You can just draw the maps onto the ground with chalks, but I think children find them much more exciting when they can combine the marks with a few objects.

Tinker trays work well for this. These are just simple baking or muffin trays, filled with an assortment of loose parts.

Tinker trays are a fantastic stimulus for building maps, which in turn lead to making marks

I would start building the maps with these as a kind of 'hook' to get the children engaged. Making marks comes second.

You can have a theme in mind when you start building the map, or you can let them decide their own ideas for creating the map.

Some great general themes are:

i) A treasure map

ii) A map of an adventure

iii) A mission

Although they are not children, here is a fantastic example of a loose parts treasure map that some very creative teachers made at a course we ran recently:

A spectacular loose parts treasure map

This would be a fantastic starting point to be enhanced with some early writing.

Get some pens or chalks and simply get to work. Some children will trace round objects, or add different features.

Children can trace, draw around, add different features, and generally build upon the physical map they have created

I think if you build it first, then adding lines second becomes much simpler.

4. Making Maps Of Stories They Know

An element of storytelling really brings to life many activities, and making a map of a story that they know well is a great way to start with maps.

As an example, here is Little Red Riding Hood:

Little Red Riding Hood's path through the forest. Watch out for the swimming sheep

All we needed for this was a piece of wood with chalkboard paint on (brilliant for mark-making), a wooden house (made out of a log), and lots of loose parts in a tinker tray.

The children have created the cottage in the woods, with the wooden stepping stones leading away from it. They have even made a stream, and a forest of pegs and feathers. There are some 'sheep' (pompoms) in the forest, and even in the stream!

Creating some kind of magical setting like this with whatever resources you have, creates an excellent backdrop to start to make marks.

With chalks the children can:

   i) Draw around the objects

   ii) Add characters, such as the wolf or Little Red Riding Hood

   iii) Draw extra features of the setting

   iv) Draw the movements of characters

   v) Make any kind of marks they like that convey some kind of meaning from
the story

5. Creating Characters

Maps can be further enhanced by using 'characters' of some sort to move
around story settings.

If you make a map of Little Red Riding Hood, for example, some kind of wolf
or woodcutter to interact with the scene really gets them more engaged, and
some writing opportunities can flow out of this.

One thing they've enjoyed doing is using pens with a characters face on the
top. For example, it might be a pen with the wolf's face on the top, and a child
is going to draw the way the wolf goes across the map.

You could have faces of characters from stories they know, or it could just be
generic story characters – like a witch, a ghost, and a princess.

Simple characters made out of play dough work really well also. Children can
draw a path they must take through a setting, or work out how a character will
find the treasure.

There are all sorts of possibilities.

20

Vehicle Writing

This chapter is particularly targeted at those more reluctant mark-makers out there.

Of course there are a huge proportion of young children that don't show the slightest bit of interest in early writing, and who can blame them! With so many other exciting activities and bits of kit on show, it makes total sense.

However, luring these children in by tapping into their interests will help to expand their horizons and hopefully get them making marks for the first time.

If I had to choose one method to attract these more reluctant children, it would definitely be vehicles.

These activities are also extremely boy-friendly, and it is often the way that there are usually a higher proportion of reluctant male mark-makers than female. Of course this is not always the case, but generally this will be the broad average of what's happening.

Hopefully these activities will kickstart their enthusiasm, and rev up their interest.

1. Attach Pens To Vehicles

The theory behind this one is extremely simple – find things that children like and attach pens to them.

Having experimented with a few different types of tape, I would say the best for the job is duct tape (much more resilient than masking tape, Sellotape or any of the others). I would also say pens are the best mark-making tool, having also tried crayons and pencils.

Tape the pens to the vehicles so that the pen-nib is touching the paper even after the lid has come off the pen.

A fire truck pen – who could resist?

You can do so many things, including:

i) Driving the vehicles over writing patterns on a big surface

ii) Use vehicles of different types and sizes – cars, trucks, trains, diggers etc

iii) Use little dinky cars with small pencils stuck on the back as a more challenging version

iv) Go down ramps

v) Have vehicles that you can rev up and drive themselves. They draw lines as if by magic! How exciting is that.

Simple ramps work a treat with these pens

It is impossible to write or draw a masterpiece with a vehicle pen, but that really isn't the point. It is about getting marks onto paper, and having fun in the process.

2. Attach Paint Brushes To Vehicles

This is the big-scale or messy version.

Huge vehicles are good for this, like big diggers or tractors.

Attach giant paint brushes to the backs of them, and then get stuck into one or all of the following activities:

i) Drive them around in the sand-pit outside. The paintbrush draws a line in the sand (as well as getting all the fabulous tyre marks from the vehicle)

ii) Put blobs of paint all over a huge piece of wallpaper and drive the vehicles around all over it

iii) Put paint on the brush and drive them down ramps

iv) Drive them through mud, dirt, glitter, or other messy substances

3. Painting With The Tyres Of Vehicles

This is more of a well-known classic activity of the repertoire, but definitely one to try out because it is loved by many children.

It's as simple as it sounds – get a range of toy vehicles, ideally with different types of tyre tracks for a bit of extra interest and stimulation.

They can dip the wheels into paint, or put blobs of colour first onto the paper you will use.

If you are feeling very arty you can control the palette – it could be two or three colours for example. Or have a seasonal theme, such as winter, with cool blues and greys. This can add depth to the narrative of what children are saying as they interact with the activity.

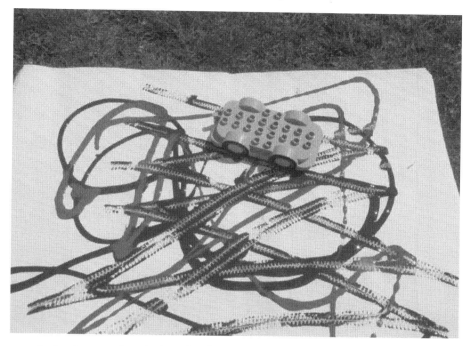

A classic way of exploring simple mark-making, texture and movement

To extend it you can try things like different writing patterns, or driving around obstacles – for example, some stones placed around the paper.

4. Painting With Wheels On Huge Paper

The scale is gradually increasing as we go through these activities, and this one is the largest of the activities, requiring a good amount of space, and a huge surface to paint on. This surface could be wallpaper, or a bed sheet, or probably a tarpaulin would work as well.

Find wheels of different descriptions. They could be:
   i) A bicycle wheel

ii) A car tyre (a real one)

iii) A tyre off a pram, pushchair, or baby stroller

iv) A scooter or tricycle tyre

Some kind of resilient painting overalls would be good for this, as this can be spectacularly messy.

Simply dip the tyres into paint that is squirted into some wide and shallow container, and then unleash them on the painting surface.

There is lots of gross motor skills meeting fine motor in this, and big scale art is brilliant for developing these two side-by-side.

5. Attach Pens To Things They Are Interested In

This idea has grown out of the original vehicle pens concept.

It is really targeted at those harder to reach children. What you do is isolate what they are really interested in, and then simply attach pens to whatever it is.

For example, why not try attaching pens to jungle animals, such as this lion:

A lion pen - raa!

A classic one is dinosaurs. I tried some T-Rexes with pens taped onto them, and we stamped them and slid them round a big piece of wallpaper.

Admittedly the pens don't last very long if you do this, but I would like to think it is an investment in getting these children doing *something.*

You can add an element of storytelling to this idea. You could, for example, make up a little narrative which the children act out. Like 'One day the T-Rexes were stamping through the forest.' (They all do lots of stamping). 'Then they came to the ice-rink and slid across.' (Lots of sliding) 'They went along the zig-zag path.'

All that kind of thing! If the children can make up their own ideas then great. If not, you just go for it, and hopefully one of two will join in.

6. Remote Control Cars With Pens Attached

Another giant piece of wallpaper would be ideal for this. Once again the pens are not going to have a very long life-expectancy, but you have to balance this with the value achieved in getting the vehicle-enthusiasts mark-making.

The simplest way is just to let them go for it! Driving forwards, backwards, and all the rest of it round the paper.

The much more advanced version is to have some kind of obstacles or road to follow, but that is much more tricky. Most children will be accessing this best at the experimenting level.

7. Beebots With Pens Attached

You can actually get a kit that attaches to the back of the beebot and makes marks as they drive around.

I imagine you've seen these beebots, but if not – they are these small bee-like robots that you program with directions by pressing buttons on the top of them. They are good on a big piece of paper in some kind of enclosed space like a tuff tray.

The writing kits are good for:
    i) Trying to draw a path from one point on the paper to the other
    ii) Freestyle mark-making (this is definitely the way to start)
    iii) Trying to draw simple shapes, such as a rectangle

8. Making Roads

This is a good one for combining small world play, construction and mark-making.

There are many ways to do this. You have some kind of large surface that the children can draw roads on, or the adults draw them originally and the children enhance it.

This is good done in a construction area, or an area where children are always playing with vehicles anyway. Some excellent ideas are:

i) Have a large wooden base with chalkboard paint on. Draw roads over the board (or the children draw them), and the children drive cars around them

ii) Children add features to a large road map on the floor

iii) Have large flat wooden blocks painted with chalkboard paint. These can be used to set down and create a road. They can draw road marking or signs on them

iv) Use wooden blocks to create buildings and vehicles along the road

21

Books For Early Writing

It's great for children to be able to see and find patterns in the things around them, and often that can be a great spark to inspire them to have a go themselves.

An excellent source of lots of visual writing patterns is the beautiful illustrations in many children's books. There are many that contain squiggles, lines, shapes, patterns, and all these other fantastic things that work so well with early writing.

I also find books can be a brilliant 'hook' for most children. They gain the interest of the majority, and draw them in.

Of course, you can't use just any books, but here are a selection of some excellent ones that have a range of different writing patterns as part of their illustrations throughout the book.

These patterns can be used as a starting point for a range of different games.

1. Cave Baby, by Julia Donaldson

In this book the baby finds a pot of paint, and creates loads of writing patterns across the wall of the cave in which he lives.

He paints a cross, a spiral, a zig-zag, a squiggle, and a few others.

Clearly a book that has been created with writing patterns in mind.

There are so many possibilities of activities you can try with this is a starting point, but here are a selection:

i) Find an ancient 'parchment' with writing patterns on (a bit of old sack would be just perfect). Can they create their own?

ii) 'Cave art' on the fence or the wall outside with chalks

iii) Big painted writing pattern art with paint, brushes and a huge paper surface

2. My Mum And Dad Make Me Laugh, by Nick Sharratt

This is my number one book to teach repeating patterns, as well as being absolutely superb for writing patterns.

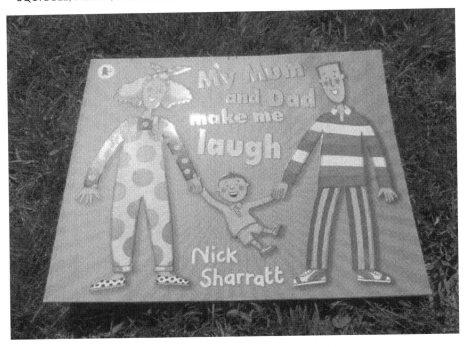

'My Mum And Dad Make Me Laugh'

Every single page is filled with multiple patterns, and examples of different lines.

To take one page at random, let's check out this picture:

Last weekend we went to the safari park. My mum put on her spottiest dress and earrings, and my dad put on his stripiest suit and tie.

I put o
"You

Every page contains multiple patterns and lines

There is so much to try to copy that is great for early writing:

The mum's dress is covered in circles.

Dad's suit is vertical lines.

The picture on the wall is wavy lines.

And so on and so on.

Throughout the book there are horizontal and vertical lines, dots, circles, spirals – all sorts going on. This book really is a treasure trove.

Some great activities include:

i) Creating collages with brightly coloured strips of paper

ii) Simple painting of the characters or settings

iii) Line drawings that copy some of the parts of the pictures

3. Owl Babies, by Martin Waddell

This beautiful, simple book has many lines in the illustrations.

For example, there are the multiple circles in the eyes of the owls. There is the feather patterns on the owls, and on their wings. There are lines on the trunks of the trees, and lots of simple leaf lines.

Pointing these out and trying to copy them in different activities really can go a long way. Some ideas include:

i) Try drawing owls on pieces of wood (this does wreck the pens a bit, but is really engaging for the less interested)

ii) Loose parts owl pictures in portrait frames with some marks added

iii) The adult draws the undulating 'u' shape feathers on giant paper, and the children cover it in loose parts or draw over it

22

Artists And Writing Patterns

One great way to initially 'hook' children's interest in writing patterns is to use famous artists.

This also has many benefits in exposing children to 'high' culture, and can be a fantastic starting point that generates talk, discussion and interest.

There are many artists that incorporate simple patterns, lines and shapes in their work. Children can experience the work of these artists, and then have a go themselves to replicate these creations through drawing, art, transient art activities, and also by using things such as loose parts.

All in all, it creates a fabulous melting pot of interweaving resources and learning.

Here are some of the best artists to try this writing pattern art with...

1. Jackson Pollock

This is probably the number one artist to show to even very young children.

Just google 'Jackson Pollock paintings' and you'll get the idea of what they look like if you've not seen them before.

Jackson Pollock was an American abstract expressionist painter, that became famous from about the 1950s onwards.

His abstract paintings are all kinds of frenetic lines, movements, squiggles, and lots of splashes of colour as well. Demonstrate what his painting looks like to the children in some way (either a printout or on a big screen), and then explore different ways of trying this squiggly mindset out.

Activities linked to it could be either adult-led, or child-led, and some good ideas are:

i) Use pipettes or turkey basters to squirt coloured water onto huge pieces of wallpaper or bed-sheets on the ground. You can also hang bed-sheets or paper on the wall. The brave amongst you might dare using squeezy water-pistols filled with paint

ii) Drizzle paint straight out of the tubes onto paper on the ground

iii) Roll balls covered in paint around in trays

iv) Squirt watery-paint out of squeezy bottles onto large surfaces

v) Create collages using loose parts or found objects such as sticks

2. Van Gogh

Van Gogh is of course a really famous artist, and it is really easy to find examples of his works online to show children.

He is particularly good for swirly lines, and also circles, zig-zags, and spirals. It all just depends on the painting that you find.

Children really enjoy the sunflowers paintings, that have many circles, triangles, and straight lines in them:

Van Gogh's 'Sunflower's are great for circles, wavy lines, and simple triangles

One brilliant painting for mark-making inspired art is 'Starry Night':

'Starry Night', by Vincent Van Gogh

This contains a range of straight lines going in different directions, spirals, swirls and circles.

Beautiful activities linked to Van Gogh paintings include:

i) If you know an adult that wouldn't mind doing this, why not give them a fake beard and they come in and pretend to be Van Gogh. There is nothing more exciting than a real-life demo of art activities than from the 'artist' themselves. It could potentially be a colleague that works with you and doesn't mind having a go, or a parent

ii) Creating starry sky huge team paintings using pens and chalks and squiggly lines

iii) Create loose parts transient art pictures with gems, coloured stones, or collage materials

iv) Create paintings and drawings of the children's own interpretations

3. Kandinsky

Google 'Wassily Kandinsky', and you will see the range of art-works that he created.

He was a Russian artist that is generally considered the founding father of abstract art.

Many of his abstract paintings are fabulous for writing patterns. They include circles, different geometric shapes such as rectangles and triangles, spirals, zig-zags, and all sorts of other lines as well.

Activities you can try out include:
    i) Collages using different shapes
    ii) Loose parts using geometric shapes – such as punk cogs, or wooden shapes
    iii) Shape arrangements of different sorts – such as using sticks
    iv) Freestyle drawing, painting, and all that kind of thing

4. A Few Select Others

Although I think I would definitely start with some of the above three artists, there are all sorts of others that you could experiment with as well.

A selection of these include:

i) *Joan Miro* - He created many colourful and child-friendly images containing a range of mark-making lines. Some paintings contain crosses, squiggles, shapes, loops, and many more. A beautiful starting point for art-led writing.

ii) *Piet Mondrian* – This guy is a good one to check out. He is the red, blue and yellow rectangle man

iii) *Pablo Picasso* – They particularly like having a go of 'crazy faces', putting the eyes, nose and lips wherever you like

23

Clothes Line Mark-Making

There are some things that children just like to do, and pegging things up onto clothes lines (washing lines) is generally one of those things.

You can target this interest with a few very creative activities that combine both fine motor and early writing with the simplistic pleasure of hanging things up.

All you need to get started is some kind of clothes line.

This could be as simple as a piece of string between two walls or two fences. You could hang one between some shelves indoors or two tables.

If you like a bit of DIY, then there are all sorts of clothes lines you can create with not much hassle. The beauty of them is that once you have made them you have them forever.

Some good DIY solutions include:
   i) Put cement into two buckets, and place two broom handles standing up vertically out of the buckets. When it is set, attach a string between the two handles
   ii) Create 'mini' clothes lines. I created some with pieces of wood, with a

hole drilled into either end. Then I superglued two pieces of dowel at either end of the wood base, and attached a string across the top
   iii) You could use a small clothes drying rack

Have a quick think about safety for outdoor clothes lines in particular. The thing to avoid is children running into them by mistake, and getting some kind of hideous neck or face injury. This is not great.

To avoid this, a few strategies that you could try include:
   i) Put clothes lines near fences or walls
   ii) Have some kind of natural barrier around it so it is not somewhere they are able to run. Something like a circle of tyres around it would work
   iii) Have the string above the height of their heads. You could have some kind of platform or step that they stand on to access the clothes line

OK, here are the activities:

1. Making Spiders Or Bugs

This is very simple this one, and great for children that only like making very few marks at one time.

Have some circles about 5 inches wide, some pens, and some clothes pegs (pins).

The children get a circle. This is going to be the spider's head and body. Draw some kind of face on the circle. Anything will be great, even just a couple of dots for eyes.

Now they are going to peg the spiders onto the clothes lines.

The spiders sit on the clothes lines, and the pegs go underneath. The pegs look like the legs of the spider.

Making bugs or spiders – an excellent way of combining fine motor skills with super simple drawing

With older ones you can try to get them to put 8 legs on, and there is lots of counting and problem solving involved.

If they are not up to counting to eight yet, just put a load of legs on! That's pretty much it.

There are many variations to this activity, some of which include:

i) They could be bugs. You have caterpillars, or ants, or anything else like that. Caterpillars would have as many legs as you could put on, and you could make really long bodies

ii) Jellyfish! Have jellyfish shaped bodies, and the pegs look like the tentacles sticking out at the bottom

2. Pirates

This is one of those great themes that most children enjoy, and it is often a good one to lure in those harder to reach boys.

You have circles of paper again, or the children could alternatively use some kind of paper or card of their choice.

The circles are going to be pirate faces. Draw on some spectacular features like bloodshot eyes, an eye patch, a gap-toothed mouth, a hairy nose, and all that kind of thing.

Now the process is similar to the spiders, only now the pegs are going to be the beards of the pirates. Put the heads so that they are sitting on the top of the washing line, and put the pegs on underneath. Loads of pegs creates a fabulous shaggy pirate beard.

A bearded pirate

Both this activity and the spiders are quite prescribed in their approach, and the children come out with a set result. However, activities like this are a great way to start children off with clothes lines. They need some ideas first to build on, and then develop some of their own ideas later on.

3. Owl Babies

I included a section on *Owl Babies* earlier in this book, and here is a fantastic clothes-line activity that you can do that links to this beautiful book.

You require some cut out pieces of paper that will be the owls. Some kind of oval shape would be good about 6 inches high.

Owls have so many wonderful writing patterns and shapes as part of their natural make-up, for example:

i) There are the concentric circle eyes

ii) They have the repeated 'u' shaped feathers

iii) They have triangle beaks

iv) There are the three forward facing toes that can be drawn as lines

v) There are the long 'u' shaped wing feathers

Children have a go at creating owls using some of these writing shapes and patterns, then they peg them on the clothes line. Once again, the owl will sit on the top of the clothes line, and pegs go underneath. You can use two pegs that will look like feet.

Owl babies sitting on the clothes line

This is a great activity for comparing size, and you can have owls of different heights.

It is also one that encourages storytelling, and children going into the narrative of the book.

4. Families

Families are crucial to all children, and make up a large part of the content of their independent mark-making and drawing.

So many children will create pictures of their parents, siblings, grandparents, pets, and anyone else closely linked to their life at home.

This super simple idea is that you create pictures of your family on bits of paper, card, or whatever else, and then peg them up on a clothes line.

This acts as a kind of picture gallery, showcasing your loved ones. It's another activity that they just like to do, and generates lots of talk amongst them about their lives at the same time.

5. Storytelling

Storytelling is a wonderful motivator to fire up children's interest across the whole curriculum.

It can definitely be harnessed for early writing with the help of a few pegs and a clothes line.

You can start them off by just pegging up pictures. Have some images from a story they know well. The children can put them on the line and talk about the story. More skilful children can try to sequence them and retell the story, but don't worry if they can't do this yet. Just pegging them up and talking is a great start!

Another way of doing it, is to have some generic story pictures. This will include characters, settings, problems, and solutions. Google 'story pictures' and something should come up.

This time the children just peg these up and try to create their own stories. Great for imagination whilst all the wonderful pegging is going on behind the scenes.

To extend it and add some mark-making, you just adapt these two strategies.

Have some small pieces of paper to write or draw on. The children can create pictures from a story that they know on them. They peg them up, and try to retell or act out the story.

The other way is that they draw generic story pictures. These could be good characters (like a dog, princess, or mouse), bad characters (like a ghost, monster, or witch). They can also draw settings (such as a castle, a mountain, or a spooky wood). A few objects or events that you might find in stories will help too (such as an apple, a key, a fire, a rainbow, and all that kind of thing).

Having some images for them to look at is a good idea to model how this whole process can be done, but hopefully some will offer their own ideas as well.

Create some pictures and then happy pegging!

24

Fine Motor Painting

Painting in any form is fantastic for fine motor control. Using brushes, rollers, even fingers, is a wonderful way of engaging children's senses and imaginations, whilst working on their muscles and coordination behind the scenes also.

You can really take the fine motor element up a notch, however, by using some carefully designed resources.

All these following activities develop all the other skills that painting stimulates (creativity, decision making etc) but they have all been specifically designed with fine motor in mind. There is a big emphasis on getting children to use their fingers and thumbs whilst using a range of mini painting utensils that are amusing, entertaining, and exciting.

1. Using Spinners

I'm sure you will have seen these types of spinners before. They are a staple of children's parties.

Children usually enjoy trying them without encouragement, which is half the battle won to start with, and you can use them for all sorts of fine motor activities.

Try some of the following:

Get a play-tray or trough, and put a shallow dusting of sand or glitter into it. Then get the children to twizz the spinners in the trays. They make lines in whatever substance you have used.

Another idea is a 'beat the clock' game. Have an egg timer, turn it over, and try to keep the spinner spinning for the time period. It's fine to pick it up and spin it again when it falls over before the time is up. A thirty second timer would be perfect for this, and maybe a one minute one at the absolute max.

The ultimate spinner activity, however, is definitely painting!

This is quite messy, just to warn you, but hours of enjoyment. It is probably best done outside.

If you have a big tuff-spot or play-tray of some description then that is perfect. What you do is put large blobs of paint all around the tray. A few different colours would be great.

Now the spinning begins!

The children are going to each have a spinner, and try to spin them in the large blobs of paint. The spinners make flailing spatter marks. In the end you will get a giant firework-style picture. Unbelievably exciting stuff!

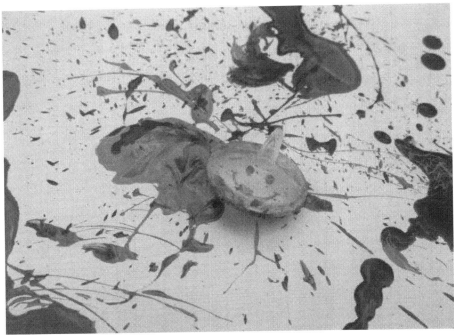

Spinners and paint – not for the faint-hearted as it's pretty messy, but a truly spectacular fine motor bonanza

Some younger children are sometimes unable to spin them very well. Never fear, however, because you can still hold the spinners, and do some dots or lines with them. Anyone can access them to some degree.

A massive bonus is that they are pretty much impossible to hold with a whole-hand grasp – they really are encouraging fingers and thumbs. This is a great prelude to holding pencils and pens.

2. Golf Tee Painters

For this you need some golf tees, a few random small objects, and some superglue.

The idea is that you stick some of the small objects to the tops of the golf tees. Some great things to stick on are any of the following:
   i) Pompoms (these fit really nicely into the curved bowl at the top)
   ii) Feathers
   iii) Cotton wool balls
   iv) Little stones
   v) Nuts or beans

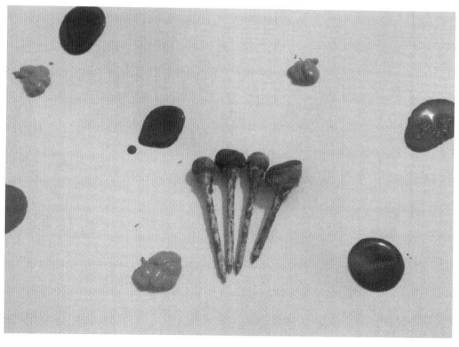

Golf tee painters

I would definitely use a strong glue for this – some kind of superglue, as you don't want the small objects to be falling off.

Then you get some paper, blobs of paint in palettes or something similar, and the children go for it!

One of the great things about this activity is that all the different golf tee painters will produce a different effect. The nuts will be a really thin line, the pompoms a thick line. The feathers will give a kind of 'feathery' line, and so on.

These are also a piece of equipment that encourage children to hold them with fingers and thumbs. A whole hand grasp is not impossible, but a bit tricky (which is what you want).

3. Vegetable Slices

Another really cheap and cheerful resource now – vegetable sticks.

All you need is some kind of vegetable that is going to be reasonably resilient when sliced up into pieces. A carrot is perfect, and this is what I always use. However, you could also use a pepper, or parsnip or potato. A mixture of these might be good to aid engagement and interest.

Small vegetable sticks really help children hold mark-making tools using just their fingers and thumb

OK, it's very simple this one. You get some paint in a palette, dip the vegetables sticks into it, and then start painting on paper.

Younger children can use really big sticks. You could even use the whole carrot.

The more skilful children are, the smaller you can make the vegetable sticks. You can even make really micro ones, and they find this an amusing challenge. The really small ones also make it impossible, once again, to hold in a whole hand grasp.

If anyone has any moral objections to using food in this way, then please just don't do this activity. However, pretty much all you need is about one carrot so it's not a massive amount of waste.

4. Clothes Pins (Pegs)

This is more of a classic fine motor activity that you may well have seen before, but I thought I should include it because it really is one of the all-time winners.

Get some clothes pins (pegs), and also a range of random objects that you can pick up with them. Some good examples might be:

   i) Cotton wool balls

   ii) Leaves – of different sizes and shapes

   iii) Pompoms

   iv) Sections of sponges cut up

   v) Pieces of material

   vi) Flowers

   vii) Plants

It's a super simple idea – the children try to put different things into the vice-part of the clothes peg, and then paint with it. Once again, you get a range of different effects with the objects you use.

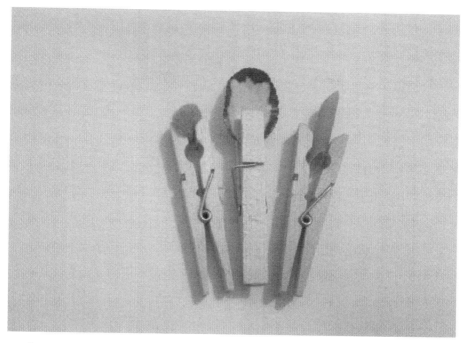

There are hundreds of objects you can find to create these DIY paint-brushes

Younger children can have the objects put into the clothes pegs for them, pre-ready when they start.

On the other hand, you can make this activity much harder by using the little tiny pegs you can get these days that are only about an inch long (or even smaller).

5. Stick Paint Brushes

This is a beautiful natural activity, great for outdoor painting, though it could also be used indoors just as easily.

Get some sticks, and attach different things to them. You can attach most things with rubber bands, wound round a few times.

A range of leaves is a beautiful way of doing this. You could also use flowers, weeds, plants, and any other natural material you can find that can be attached to the end of the stick.

Stick paint-brushes – a beautiful and natural activity

You could also use man-made objects, such clothes pegs, pipe cleaners, toy animals, dinosaurs – or anything else you can think of!

What child wouldn't want to paint with a T-Rex stuck to the end of a stick!?

Older or more skillful children may be able to try to attach the objects to the sticks using pipe cleaners. This really brings excitement and ownership to what they have made.

25

Final Thoughts

And with that we have reached the end.

I hope now you are fully equipped with all the exciting activities you could ever need to get children making marks, and developing their fine motor skills in the most positive and effective way they can.

A quick recap of some key summaries:
i) Remember the boys - motivate them and everyone will be on side
ii) Make everything child-friendly
iii) Use stories and drama to bring activities to life
iv) Use sports and competitions and games
v) Identify their interests and use them
vi) Use secret missions and spies
vii) Use unicorns and dinosaurs and superheroes
viii) Be creative and have fun

Along with the content of this book, I am delighted to offer you a selection of bonus materials completely for free. These can be found at https://earlyimpactbooks.com/bonus/

They include:

-101 Fine Motor/Early Writing Games Cheat Sheet

-Bonus Video - Magical Ways To Use Pipettes For Fine Motor

-5 Bonus Genius Fine Motor Ideas (not included in this book)

If you want to share the ideas in this book with colleagues, then I have also put together a practical video training version of it. This is a paid product, and is particularly beneficial as a team-training event.

I have kept the time down to 2 hours so it's perfect for inhouse training. There are 25 hands-on, practical videos that showcase the ideas in this book using real life resources.

You can check out the training course here - https://earlyimpactlearning.com/squiggle-101/

If you have enjoyed this book, I would be so grateful if you could leave a review on Amazon. These reviews really help to promote the book to a wider audience, and hopefully spread the impact that these ideas can have.

Now go ahead and start TODAY!

Good luck, and best wishes!!

THE END

P.S. Please remember to download your free book if you haven't done so already. You can find it here: https://earlyimpactbooks.com/50-games/

Your Free Book Is Waiting

About the Author

Martin Williams is the founder of the training company Early Impact. He has worked in early education in the UK for ten years, teaching children between the ages of 3 and 5. He is driven by a determination to make early learning exciting and engaging for both children and adults.

In his work with Early Impact, he has trained thousands of teachers and practitioners in many of the key areas of education. He has delivered school improvement projects for authorities, and he has led training for local early years quality teams.

He blogs and writes about all the educational topics he believes he can make a difference in, and he is strongly committed to sharing information and helping others as much as he can. You can find his blog by going to earlyimpactlearning.com

He is passionate about the 'practical' nature of learning both for adults and children. All of his courses are fast-paced, interactive, and contain a multitude of real-life resources that attendees try out.

He runs hands-on training courses in face-to-face venues across the North of England and the Midlands, specializing in early phonics, mathematics, fine motor and mark-making.

He delivers popular online training sessions through Early Impact's website which you can find here - earlyimpactlearning.com/online-courses/

Also by Martin Williams

Other books include...

101 Games To Play Whilst Socially Distancing
The Amazon #1 Bestseller in the UK.

Attempting social distancing with young children raises many questions: how is it possible? How can we incorporate it into games and activities? How do we help and support children with this lack of human connection? These are the questions that this book answers.

Split into 12 areas of the curriculum, this book offers 101 scintillating games to play in the context of social distancing for children aged 3-7.

Reviews

Rosie on Amazon

I have been on several of Martin's courses...and been blown away by all the ideas and suggestions he has for Early Years. This book is no different!! Superb!
  Rosie, Review on Amazon

I am so excited about this book!! This book is a GODSEND. It is so well written and well structured, so easy to read... I wholeheartedly endorse it. I love the way the author has included the educational aspects of the game, and appropriate elements of developmental psychology. Such a handy resource!!
  Sunshan, Review on Amazon

Loose Parts Play – A Beginner's Guide

Looking to unleash the powerful learning potential of loose parts play, but don't know how to begin...

Loose parts play offers a magical and wonder-filled way to deliver learning across the whole curriculum. But there are many things you need to know to get started on the correct footing (and many things that will go wrong if you don't)...

What is loose parts play? What are its benefits? How do you set it up? Where do you find ideas? How can it make a real IMPACT?

Bursting with more than 200 practical ideas, activities and provocations, 'Loose Parts Play – A Beginner's Guide' is the perfect handbook for teachers and parents of children aged 0-5 that are looking to develop an outstanding loose parts curriculum either at work or at home.

Reviews

I particularly like that this is a child-led approach and that the resources are simple everyday objects. It is great to see the imagination and creativity it encourages in our pupils - this is the reason why most of us entered the profession. This is a brilliant book and I will be digesting its ideas for some time.
    Gregg, Review on Amazon

Excellent insight into loose parts play. Explains the purpose and how it can be used in children 0-5, but also applies to older children too. Accessible for both teachers and parents, lots of inspiring ideas and examples. Wish I had read this for my children! Would highly recommend.
    Nicky L, Review on Amazon

Printed in Great Britain
by Amazon